GRITTY.

ii

GRITTY.

A Book Written By First Generation
Students For First Generation Students

Dr. Rodney Lewis
Ron Lewis

GRITTY. (Black)

ISBN-13: 978-1494201692

ISBN-10: 1494201690

GRITTY. (White)

ISBN-13: 978-1499525441

ISBN-10: 1499525443

BISAC: Education / Student Life & Student Affairs

Printed in the United States of America.

GRITTY.

A BOOK WRITTEN BY FIRST GENERATION STUDENTS FOR FIRST GENERATION STUDENTS

BY DR. RODNEY LEWIS **AND** RON LEWIS

This book is dedicated to first generation students all over the world.

If we can do it, you can do it.

Thank you, mom and dad. The both of us are gritty because of you!

GRITTY.

A BOOK WRITTEN BY FIRST GENERATION STUDENTS FOR FIRST GENERATION STUDENTS

THE LEWIS INFLUENCE

BY DR. RODNEY LEWIS AND RON LEWIS

Cover Art:
Anthony "The Wizard" Stewart

Lewis Influence Logo:
Anthony "The Wizard" Stewart

Editor:
Jessica Montalvo

TABLE OF CONTENTS

Introduction

*"Education is not the preparation for life,
Education is life."*
-John Dewey

We could see our dad's face as he walked through the door. It was in slow motion as he arrived home from work. He stepped in the house with a semi-smile on his face...

POW...POW...

"GET DOWN!" our dad yelled waving his big right paw in the downward motion. Our mother, father, sister, and the both of us hit the floor.

We heard...
...POW...POW...POW...POW...POW...
SCCCRRRRRHHHHHHHH!

Drive-bys were a common place in St. Louis, Missouri. Life on the north side of St. Louis was flooded with crime, drugs, and gangs. Think about growing up in a neighborhood where if you wore the wrong color or your hat the wrong way, your life could vanish.

Commonly, gang signs were a way to communicate. You did not need to be the sharpest knife in the kitchen to understand if you saw the same car driving around your block more than once that usually ended with negative outcomes. Use your imagination. Despite living near condemned buildings, liquor stores, and Chop Sueys, our grittiness moved us forward.

See, the twins are not above you or below you, but instead we are you! The both of us understand some of your living environments are rough which may make pursuing or attending college difficult. Just understand, you will have to push like you have never pushed before. If you hang on long enough, you can make your wildest dreams come true. The both of us are living proof.

Growing up, our parents worked their butts off every day. Our mom worked in a factory for over thirty years and never went higher than an elementary school education. Our father was an excellent chef. However, he did not attend a culinary arts school. Actually, our father is a high school dropout. To be real with you, if you check out stats on kids like us, we should have never made it out of St. Louis. Our parents had very little "book" education and we grew up in an unsafe neighborhood. You do the math.

Our parents were gritty, though. Watching them work hard, for thirty plus years ignited our fire. They taught us the true meaning of hard work and hustle. We bet if you looked hard enough, you have a gritty person in your life. Stand on the shoulder of a giant and let them show you how it is done. Why? Because, for us, watching our parents wake up at 4:00 a.m., hearing how physical their jobs were, and observing them go to bed tired and worn out, made college small potatoes. Our thought was, "If mom and dad can do this, we most certainly can do that!"

What does it mean to be gritty? Simple. Grit is having the strength and resilience to overcome your obstacles and reach your goals. Sounds simple, right? However, how will you respond to your long-time friends when they are enticing you to participate in activities, which will have you talking with the cops early and often? Will you be gritty enough to part ways with them? How gritty will you be when you receive your test back and your test grade is a 58%? Will you call the teacher an idiot and drop the class, give up, and accept your failing grade? Or push yourself to study like you have never studied before?

To be gritty, you have to care more about succeeding than your possible failures. Your grit is a gut check! It forces you to dig deep in your pain and believe you are going to accomplish your goals. College is a tough task if you are going hard at it. Plus, if you are challenging yourself in the classroom by reading, studying, and asking questions, your college experience will not be easy, but worth it.

To make it worth it, you have to be gritty! Listen to us, there is nothing extra special about Rodney and Ron Lewis. We have come from unsafe neighborhoods, low test scores, and self-doubt. If we can make it through losing a college scholarship because of too much partying, or sleeping in class and not feeling smart enough, we know you can do it.

14's

It was the winter of 1998 on a Saturday morning. We were pacing nervously, with sweaty palms. We sat in that high school classroom thinking the start of our college career hangs on this double-digit number. This sucks! As we were taking the test, we were feeling stupid, unprepared, and wondering if we were cut out for college life. This ACT was going to break us.

To be considered for a four-year university, we needed, at the time, a score of 18. The questions were hard, and we thought we had to be dumb for not knowing this stuff! Once the both of us received our scores of a 14, we were not feeling intelligent. The twins studied and took the test again. Things will be different if we studied longer, we thought. Yeah right!

GRITTY.

The both of us got 14's again. Yes, we were officially dumb and dumber! We have learned in the grand scheme of things, those 14's did not matter. We started our college experience at St. Louis Community College at Meramec in St. Louis, Missouri. We worked hard and finished our bachelor's degrees at Barry University. The both of us did not stop there. We have masters' degrees and Rodney has his doctorate while Ron is finishing his up. Nothing could stop us, but us!

It does not make a difference what your GPA is, what your SAT or ACT score is, or what you score on your college entrance exam. Scores did not define us, and scores will not define you. Your grittiness, when it is all said and done, will define your college career. Both of us were horrible at College Algebra; horrible. Maybe it is a twin thing? Who knows! Needless to say, test after test; we received D's and a few F's. How would you show your grittiness?

The Math Lab was a place where students could receive immediate help with math, all-day, every day. There were three older women in the lab and they knew their stuff! They were sort of crabby, but we appreciated their patience and willingness to make sure we understood our work. Every day, after class, we would walk to the lab, get our books, papers, pencils, and CD players out, and start to work.

While the 2Pac and Jay-Z thumped in our headphones, we were doing math problems and asking for assistance when needed. We could have gone to McDonald's or Taco Bell/ Pizza Hut for lunch, but instead, we studied like crazy because we were better than D's and F's. We got gritty! If you want to graduate college at a high level, it is mandatory that you get gritty. Before you know it, graduation will be staring you in the face and you will either look at your time as a big waste or four years well spent. Remember, time is moving with or without you.

Looking Ahead

Welcome to the start of this journey. Just so you know, this book was written exactly for you, the student. This was not written for your professors, counselors, or academic advisors. Sure, we would like for them to read it, but this book is for the first generation college student. We know who you are, because we are you. No lie! A first generation college student is described as being the first in their immediate family to attend college and having parents who did not graduate with a bachelor's degree. So, if your tenth cousin, Pookie Williams III, graduated college, you are still a first generation college student...just saying.

You have a lot riding on those young shoulders, such as being the first in your family to graduate college, leaving your friends and family, and in some cases, you may feel as if you are not smart enough. Take it from us, we have felt it all. This is why your grittiness is so important. It will push you past these obstacles toward your success. Our parents, as great as they were, could not help us with the college process. To be honest with you, it did not matter, though. That was not going to be an excuse. These two inner city boys were determined to make it work. For you, you can make this happen as well. This is truly your time to make history and that is what you are going to do one way or another.

Remember, this is about keeping your eyes on the prize. This has nothing to do with how good you look. Real talk: putting energy into your shoes, hair, and clothes more than studying is the opposite of gritty. Chapter 1 tells you to *Stop Shining and Start Grinding!*

In Chapter 2, we are asking you to be you! A lot of first generation students come from the same neighborhoods we were brought up in. Yet, some of your friends, and maybe you, are more concerned with fitting in, instead of standing out. You will never be successful if you are looking to simply fit in; you are not being yourself. Drop your *Swag,* which means, take off the "costume" and show the world who you really are.

GRITTY.

We help you understand very clearly in Chapter 3 why it is important to *Know The Right Numbers.* You know, it is cool to know how many followers you have on Twitter and Instagram or how many friends you have on Facebook, but, you better know what your GPA is and how many credits you need for your major. You have to take ownership in your numbers.

When you *Play With Dogs, You Get Fleas.* In Chapter 4, we want you to understand you are as good as the company you keep. It is an old motto, but it is still powerful today. You are about to do something special with your life. Who will be there to see it?

Do you realize that you are attending college for someone else? Yes, Chapter 5 will explain why you are learning and studying to support others. In short, *This Is Not For You.*

Chapter 6 simply gets you ready for your future job and gently brings it all home.

At the end of each chapter, we have created a reflective guide to help you think about what you just read and assist you in developing your gritty mindset. To get the most out of the chapter, answer the questions, understand yourself, and understand your level of grittiness.

Let's Do This

We are excited that you are taking this journey with us. We are about to change your life because we are about to help you look at your own grittiness differently; Straight up!
Listen, maybe you are hanging around some people who are not helping you move forward and need some advice on how to move on. We got you! You might not get the support from your family and need two tall twins to lean on. We got you! Understand, this book has you covered.

Remember, this book is for you, the first generation college student. Just know we are proud of you. We know what you are feeling and some of the hesitation you might experience. It's all good. We can go through this together. At the same time, this book holds no punches. The concept of college can be scary and intimidating, but more than doable! College is not above you, but for you.

Therefore, if you feel uncomfortable reading this book, that is good. That means we are speaking to you and you are feeling it.

Lastly, we will provide personal experiences to help guide you through the college process. Once you complete this book, the real work begins. Reading this is great, awesome, fine, and dandy, but you have to apply what you have learned. Seriously, it takes grittiness to look at who you are and make changes, but no one can do it for you. You will have to do that yourself.

Laying The Foundation

Before you start reading, it is important to comprehend the foundation of this book. As you will read, we experienced roadblocks during our college career. We earned low ACT scores, lost a scholarship, and tanked our GPA. We invested more into our appearance than academics, questioned our intelligence in the classroom, valued the nightlife more than college life, and took several remedial courses in college. Through all of those obstacles, poor decisions, and challenges, we never gave up. We were knocked down numerous times and we had reasons to stay down, but we owned three principles in college that made us stand up! Today, personally and professionally, we continue to apply these three principles to keep us gritty during our darkest hours. The foundation of The Lewis Influence and this book is built upon three principles that have proven to be the backbone of our grittiness.

Belief, Faith, and Fight

These three simple, but powerful, words have supported us during our undergrad, grad, and post grad degrees. You see, we were not 4.0 students in high school or college. We just had the belief we would graduate. Regardless, if we received A's or F's, we had the deep-down belief we would succeed. Did this belief waver at times? Sure! But we never quit our educational journey.

To be gritty, your belief is the flame that keeps your inner fire burning. You are going to face some rough times during your college years, but don't stop believing in your dreams. As you progress through the book, you will soon realize that you own your education. We mean, "Own it." Not only do you own your education, but also you are the pilot and captain of your journey. As the captain and pilot, you have to utilize the power of belief to help guide you to your destination. Will you reach your destination, Captain? Ask your faith.

Consider faith as your vision for the future that only you can see. For example, you believe you will receive an A in math if you study hard and ask for help when needed. On the other hand, your faith is that by attending college, you will have a successful future.

Faith is taking a step when you cannot see the stairs. Sometimes, when things are going downhill, your faith takes a hit. Like you, our faith has been tested over and over. Some days you are going to be walking on cloud nine. Other days, you may question the purpose of attending college or if you will get a job after graduation. When friends, family, professors, and others lose faith in you, have faith in you.

If you learn to depend on your faith often and early, you will be able to make it through anything and everything. As college graduates, our FAITH helped us to see the unseen things. We knew we were going to graduate and achieve our goals thereafter. It didn't come as quickly and easily as we would have liked, but we still managed to achieve our goals. Our parents instilled in us a relentless belief: we understand that there's nothing we can't achieve. Our faith in our goals and dreams are deeply rooted in our gritty mentality, which gives us enough strength to fight.

If you want to be gritty, you have to be willing and ready to fight for your college education. This is our last cornerstone of grittiness. If you are reading this book, you have a fighting spirit. We fought to merely receive a decent math grade. You will fight for your belief and the faith in yourself. There are going to be close friends and family who are going to question your education, and you have to be willing to fight those questions. College is not easy. Trust us; only the strong survive in the big leagues. If college were easy, every college and university would have a 100% graduation rate, but that is not the case. The fight you develop toward your education will be the same exact fight you will need for the rest of your life.

Being gritty is hard work on top of hard work. When you are gritty, you know that bumps and bruises are part of the journey. Only the gritty students are able to fight through the pain, wavering confidence, lack of support, and limited resources. When you are gritty, you know there is no free lunch in the free world. Instead, we will wake up earlier, go to bed later, study more, party less, attend tutoring sessions everyday, and we will never give up on ourselves. When you are ready to fight, it is a commitment to you personally, but also, it is a commitment to all of the people that have helped you along the way.

Every chapter in this book is built on the belief in yourself, faith in your dreams, and the willingness to fight for your future.

Are You Gritty?

Reflect

Describe your current living environment.

_____

_____

_____

_____

_____

_____

_____

_____

_____

_____

Describe your dream living environment.

_____

_____

_____

_____

_____

_____

_____

_____

_____

_____

_____

Name five ways how developing a GRITTY attitude can help you achieve your dream living environment.

_____
_____
_____
_____
_____
_____
_____
_____
_____
_____

14's

Name a class or a subject that you are struggling in.

_____
_____
_____

What three realistic changes are you willing to make tomorrow to improve your grade?

_____
_____
_____
_____
_____
_____
_____

Looking Ahead
What does it mean to be a college student?

_____

_____

_____

_____

_____

_____

_____

_____

_____

_____

_____

_____

List three potential obstacles you might
face in college?

_____

_____

_____

_____

_____

_____

_____

_____

_____

_____

_____

_____

_____

List three ways you are going to overcome
your three obstacles?

_____

_____

_____

_____

_____

_____

_____

_____

_____

_____

_____

_____

Belief, Faith, and Fight

Do you believe you are going to accomplish
your dreams? Give three reasons why.

_____

_____

_____

_____

_____

_____

_____

_____

_____

_____

GRITTY.

After reading our definition of faith, how has faith helped you overcome the tough times in your life?

_____

_____

_____

_____

_____

_____

_____

_____

_____

_____

_____

_____

_____

_____

_____

_____

_____

_____

_____

_____

_____

_____

_____

_____

_____

Describe a time when you had to fight for success? What did you learn about yourself?

_____
_____
_____
_____
_____
_____
_____
_____
_____
_____
_____
_____
_____
_____
_____
_____
_____
_____
_____
_____
_____
_____
_____
_____

Chapter 1
Stop Shining & Start Grinding

"There are no shortcuts to any place worth going."
-Beverly Sills

"Ummm, let me see...I think I will wear the red bandanna with the red and black J's and the all-white Jordan jersey with no t-shirt!" It was our freshman year at St. Louis Community College at Meramec and let us tell you, there were two things on our mind: looking good and pretty girls.

Political Science class was boring to us. We sat in the front row of the class pretending to pay attention. The professor had a monotone voice and after fifteen minutes of hearing it, our eyes got heavy. We knew one thing: we were the best-looking dudes in class. There was more time spent trying to look like Jay-Z (in the early 2000's) than understanding how politics work in this country.

Yes, we would match our shirts, hats, shoes, jerseys, socks, chains, do-rags, shorts, pants, t-shirts, and belts. Everybody wants to look nice. Who doesn't? We are not saying you should walk out of your house looking a hot mess. However, we are saying more importance should be placed on dominating the classroom instead of your fashion game. Remember that Political Science course we told you about? This is how we studied for this class:

Rodney: "Hey Twin, I think that dude over there took the test in the 8:00 a.m. class!"
Ron: "Let's go ask him about the test! If he helps us out, that gives us an hour to study."
Rodney: "Cool!"

Those are the study techniques that will get you to Harvard, baby! Not! Time after time, we were invested in trying to get something for nothing. The both of us tried to master ways to get easy grades instead of taking the time to study and learn. We realized there are no shortcuts to success.

Do not behave like us; start getting gritty in your college classroom on day 1. Then, keep grinding in the classroom on day 2, 32, 64,129 and so on! As brothers, we did not realize the opportunity we had in front of us. There was no understanding of what college was going to mean for two city boys from St. Louis. For a while, we just took going to college for granted.

Now, at 33 years old, we understand we used our time for the wrong things. Yes, we looked good, but some of our grades looked terrible. As freshmen, we had little to no grittiness, and it was all about the bright lights of the clubs and meeting the ladies. Real talk: start with a different plan. You can be the freshest person in class with the worst grades. Your new shoes will not mean squat when your F is staring you in the face. Be true to your purpose for attending college and understand what you "want" and what you "expect."

Wants vs. Expectations

We have witnessed many students enter college "wanting" to be a doctor, lawyer, or engineer. Students go to college and want to achieve good grades. Most graduate and want an excellent job, slick home, and smooth car. This is great! After all, if you've spent four years working hard in college, then you deserve to have some of the things that you "want."

"Wanting" good grades, a dream job, a slick home, and a beautiful car is a good look! You have the right to want as much as you want. As we talk with students, we have realized some are just "wanting" things to happen instead of "expecting" things to happen.

You see, you can want to be in a certain profession or industry, but if you don't expect it to become a reality...well, it won't. Your expectations will drive you to study harder and longer. Those mighty expectations will make you wake up early and focused and end the night hungry for more. When you receive a bad grade on a test, your expectations will make you re-evaluate your study habits and guide you to the professor's office for extra support. That is expecting success. Ron illustrated this point when a middle school student did not expect to be a doctor, but merely wanted it.

While volunteering for a middle school reading program, Ron asked the students to tell him their name and future profession. One young lady stated her name and told Ron she wanted to be a heart doctor. So, Ron started to breakdown what it took to become a heart doctor. He outlined the immaculate grades she would need in high school to be accepted into an outstanding college. Next, he explained, in college, not only did she need exceptional grades, she needed to pass the MCAT (the medical school assessment test) in order to get accepted into medical school.

Finally, Ron discussed the nearly twelve to fourteen years of schooling it would take for her to reach her goal of becoming a doctor. Once he completed his overview, the middle school student stated, "I changed my mind, I want to be something else."

This middle schooler simply "wanted" to be a doctor, but it was not her "expectation." It sounds amazing to hear students speak about their lofty goals for their future. The follow up question is, "Do you expect to have what you want?" Again, if you expect to reach your goals, you will be willing and ready to do whatever it takes to make it happen.

One way we can tell if students really expect to reach the goals they want is by looking at their grades. You can't expect to be an engineer if you fail your engineering courses. Without passing those courses and gaining the knowledge, it will be impossible to become an engineer. As you will read later, when you graduate with a major, your graduation means you are knowledgeable in that field of study. Your knowledge tells the world that you are ready to make a contribution to the industry you studied during your four years of college.

What we are telling you is to move past the wanting and live in the expecting phase. Drop the "I want this to happen" talk, and instead, tell yourself, "I expect this to happen!" A wise person said, "No one can rise to low expectations." Therefore, if your wants are high, but your expectations are low, then you will never reach your wants. On the other hand, if you raise your expectations, you better be ready to grind for every want you have.

Grind For Everything

Let's get serious. Some of you are not putting in enough work in the classroom. You have lofty goals of what you want to achieve, but you are too busy chasing the opposite sex and/or just kicking it. You will not be given anything and will only earn the grade you receive.

We have seen students looking good with their matching clothes. But really, in ten years, your clothes will mean nothing to your future. Nothing! College is the big league. The professor is not calling your house to ask why you did not attend class. Your mommy and daddy can't call the professor and check on your grades during the midterm. That F you received is your F! We are asking you to own every moment and make the most of it. This is an opportunity of a lifetime and you will have to grind for everything.

Take all of your courses seriously, from drawing to biology. If you are looking to match something, instead of clothes and shoes, make sure those grades match your expectations. While it may be easy to get an A in Drawing 101, that grade may be harder to come by in biology. The question in both courses would be, "What do you expect?" Showing grittiness is studying and earning the very best grades you can achieve against all odds. The key words here are the "very best grades you can achieve." If you are earning a few C's in your courses and put everything into that grade, we salute you. For some of you though, that is not the case and you know it.

A few of you understand your grades could be better. If you were grinding every day, your grades would be higher. We are telling you if you can earn all A's, then your GPA should be a 4.0 every semester. Would you settle for a B when you could earn an A? Why would you settle for a C when you know you could earn a B? This is where your grittiness kicks in. It is easy to earn a C, but you know you are capable of earning a B. You will have to overcome that "mental flea" and earn the B. Mentally, that is the grit and the everyday hustle is the grind. This made much more sense once we started working on our masters and doctorates.

Early in our college career, we earned the quickest grade that required the least amount of effort. Where were the grit and the grind? It was on the Sega Dreamcast, PlayStation (we know, we are old!), and the club. We did not want to study and put forth the extra effort. We wanted A's and B's, but had no expectation for that to occur. By second semester of our first year, our grades slipped big time and we were looking at each other confused!

GRITTY.

You may say, "But why should I care that much about grades? You guys have master's degrees and doctorates! It will not matter in the long run." See, that is exactly what we thought back in the day. And to a certain degree, we were right! Your grades will not matter in the long run. We have gotten jobs and not one employer has looked at transcripts.

But here is where we were wrong. While grades never earned us a job, it created those success habits that we still use today. Understand, grit is the ability to endure consistent obstacles and build successful habits. Grind is your everyday actions to build those habits. A quick example would be, for our jobs, we must develop high-quality reports to our supervisors regarding student performance. Sure, we could slop the reports together and provide the minimum suggested. However, much like working on our master's and doctorates, we go above and beyond the recommended because we expect when our name is on a document, it equates to excellence.

What happens when your grit is low and your grind is absent? What happens when you want the wrong things and expect nothing? You think you are the man and you hit up the club, often!

Kirby's

How could we not look forward to Wednesday nights? They used to be special! Why? It was College Night at Kirby's, which was one of the hottest nightclubs in St. Louis, Missouri. This club attracted students from many of the local colleges such as St. Louis University, University of Missouri St. Louis (UMSL), and Lindenwood University. There were young people attending from other cities in Missouri and some who did not attend college. Needless to say, on Wednesdays, the place was packed wall-to-wall.

Kirby's was amazing! You would see a girl on campus during the day with big shoes, big hair, and bifocals. Then, once she got in the club with banging music, strobe lights, and high energy, she looked like a super model by the end of the night. Well that may be a bit of an exaggeration, but this place attracted some of the prettiest girls in St. Louis.

Our first semester of college, we went to the club twice a month, maybe three. By second semester, BOOM! The addiction started! We started going out 4x's a month. When we would meet girls on Wednesdays, we would go on dates with them on the other six days during the week. It was highly possible for us to enjoy the nightlife three to four nights a week!

GRITTY.

The human body needs sleep, right? And when you are partying during the week and getting no sleep, where do you think this sleep took place? Yes, you guessed it; in class. Since we did not take college too seriously, on Thursdays, we slept during sociology and astronomy. We were in the front row 'knocked...out!'

The both of us got by with C's in both of those classes. Lucky us! In another way, we were not so lucky. Our low grit and absent grind cost us a $2,500 scholarship. In order to keep the scholarship, every semester we had to maintain a 2.5 GPA. At the end of our first semester, one of us earned a 3.2 and the other earned a 3.4. Once the second semester ended, because of our poor study habits, studying girls, and the nightlife, Ron earned a 1.7 and Rodney earned a 2.3 GPA.

Take ownership of your learning as if your life depended on it. Your life really does depend on your education. Because of this independence, you must expect success from yourself. The both of us wanted good grades, but did not fully expect them. However, we wanted to go to the club and expected ourselves to go. Our priorities were jacked up! Getting past this roadblock was tough for us. We had horrible grades and lost money. It was the first time we truly struggled in school. To get things back in shape, we got gritty, started grinding in every class, and powered through.

Power Through

One of the most important challenges in college is powering through mountains and roadblocks, which get in your way. Some students just quit. You have to be ready to power through. You have to be willing to get up when you get knocked down over and over again. We will tell you this repeatedly; college is not easy. It is not designed to be easy. If it were easy, this country would have the most college graduates in the world. Part of the daily grind is powering through all of the difficult obstacles you encounter. Yes, you want success, you expect it, you are grinding hard with studying and working, but when life takes a strange twist and deals you a bad hand, you have to power through.

Don't let anything or anyone stop you. You may feel like you are not getting the support from your professors, but don't stop going to class. You have too much riding on your college education. As we will explain, someone is depending on you to get your education. If you quit, what are you going to tell the person who was looking at you? This is your chance and opportunity to change generations and future generations in your family. Power through.

Your ability to power through your toughest
challenges will be important if you are going to
complete your college education. It may take
you four, eight, or even twelve years to
complete your degree. In reality, it does not
matter one bit. Here is a little secret, there are
no completion dates on a college degree.
Therefore, regardless if you graduate in four or
eight years, we are all college graduates. So,
every time you hit a bump in the road, just get
up, keep it moving and...power through. Never
stay on the ground when you fall. Again, get
back up with possible tears in your eyes,
bruised knees and hands, and power through.
As we mentioned earlier in the chapter, you
have to expect success and not just want it. If
you can learn to power through, then you will
be unstoppable...Rodney did.

Dr. Gritty

Rodney never thought he was smart enough,
bright enough, or intelligent enough as a kid.
After finishing his second master's degree, he
understood his next big challenge. He wanted
to complete his doctorate degree. The mere
fact he had arrived at this point in his schooling
was a blessing. He hated reading and writing
all throughout his undergraduate and graduate
studies. Yet, there was a challenge in doing
something he thought was forbidden for
someone like him. Rodney never thought he
was a critical thinker on most things outside of

playing basketball. Because he felt it was challenging for him to enroll in a doctoral program, he decided to give it a leap of faith.

He spent two weeks gathering his letters of recommendation, writing and responding to essays, and putting together his resume and letters of interest. Rodney was nervous and excited all at once. When the paperwork was complete, he went to Walmart and bought some expensive plastic covers to secure his documents. He wanted to look professional and doctoral! Finally, Rodney put everything together and drove to the university and delivered it in person. He saw himself graduating from this institution as Dr. Rodney S. Lewis.

A week later, he received a letter from the university. Just looking at the envelope made his heart pound a thousand beats per minute! Before Rodney opened the letter, he envisioned it saying he was accepted into the school. The excitement and anxiety wrapped the letter into his sweaty palms. Like a mad man, Rodney fanatically ripped open the letter. After reading the first line, the poor guy's heart sank, and his bald-head dropped. It did not say, "Congratulations!" To sum up the letter, it said the writing samples he provided needed extra attention and if he desired, he could re-apply within a week or two. While Rodney was disappointed, he was not discouraged. The young educator thought, "I will just have more people look at the samples and everything will be fine." So quickly, he rewrote and sent his writing samples to his sister and a friend.

Rodney had them read his essays and they provided him with valuable feedback. He felt there was no way they were going to deny him this time. Rodney returned to Walmart to buy fancier plastic covers, and again, drove to the university to submit for the second time. Rodney was more confident his second time around than his first.

The school told him he would hear within a few weeks and sure enough he did. On a cold day in November, there was a letter from the university. Rodney's heart started beating twice as fast. He saw the letter and because he and his wife were entertaining family, he took the letter upstairs to his bedroom. The letter was ripped open. Rodney was nervous, excited, confident, and worried. After reading a few lines, his head dropped with pain, and his worst fears had come true. He was not going to attend this university for his doctorate. The letter stated his writing samples were not on a "doctoral level." To make matters worse, the earliest he could re-apply to this school would be in a year. Crushed! Tears started running down Rodney's face.

GRITTY.

In his eyes, this letter proved he was not smart enough. Rodney sat on his bed and read the rejection letter over and over, hoping each time he read it, the words would magically change to congratulate him on his acceptance. However, the more he read it, the more reality set in.

Rodney was determined not to give up. He started thinking, "If writing is my biggest problem, then I need to become better at it." So the day after receiving his second rejection letter, he went to Borders and bought *English Grammar For Dummies*. Every night, Rodney sat with his wife. And as she surfed the web or watched TV, he worked in this grammar book.

He saw "Dr. Lewis" printed every night before he closed his eyes. To improve his understanding of basic grammar, Rodney would write sentences and paragraphs for extra practice. Along with this grinding, he gained a love for reading and started reading so much that he noticed two bonus rewards: *1. His writing instantly improved because of his increased exposure to new vocabulary and sentence organization. 2. He noticed all of the grammar he was studying in his workbook was applied in the books he was reading.* With every book finished and extra writing practice completed, his confidence grew. He was determined to conquer his fear and felt if he received another opportunity to enroll, he would be more than prepared.

Three months after being told he was not good enough, Rodney was entertaining the idea again. However, this time, the new university had a reputation of being one of the best in Missouri. Rodney embraced the challenge. Two weeks prior to enrolling, he received all the necessary information regarding the program. He previewed his writing prompts and outlined his answers carefully. This young man was stronger, hungrier, and more prepared than his first two attempts. This time around, instead of wanting to get accepted, this next opportunity would show that he expected to get accepted.

Now, here was the moment of truth! Rodney did the writing, communicating, and reading. Two weeks after submitting his paperwork for acceptance, the mail arrived and unlike last time, he was not worried or fearful. On this day, what he wanted and expected merged into something beautiful. Across the top of the letter, where the introduction started, it read, "Congratulations!" What a feeling! Rodney did the unthinkable, his unthinkable. He was officially accepted into a doctoral program.

What happens when you are mentally gritty, grinding daily, and powering through? You become a Doctor of Education at 29 years of age. You have the same qualities as Rodney,

GRITTY.

and he is no different than you. Remember,
stop shining and start grinding!

Reflect

Wants vs. Expectations

What are your three "wants" in life?

_____

_____

_____

_____

_____

_____

_____

_____

_____

_____

_____

_____

Now, name three ways you will transform those wants into expectations? Be honest!

_____

_____

_____

_____

_____

_____

_____

_____

_____

_____

Grind For Everything

Name three ways you can grind in your school work? (Don't say work harder and study) Be specific and honest!

_____
_____
_____
_____
_____
_____
_____
_____
_____
_____
_____
_____
_____
_____
_____
_____

What class are you settling in right now? Why are you settling? If you did not settle, what grade would you have in that class?

_____
_____
_____
_____
_____

_____
_____
_____
_____
_____
_____

Power Through

What issue, class, or obstacle do you think you
will have to power through to be successful
in college?

_____
_____
_____
_____
_____
_____
_____
_____
_____
_____
_____
_____
_____
_____
_____
_____
_____
_____

GRITTY.

Remember a time when you had to power through. Answer the following questions:

Who supported you as you powered through your obstacle?

_____
_____
_____
_____
_____
_____
_____
_____
_____
_____
_____
_____
_____
_____

Why did you need to power through?

_____
_____
_____
_____
_____
_____
_____
_____
_____

GRITTY.

_____
_____
_____
_____
_____
_____
_____
_____

How did you power through?

_____
_____
_____
_____
_____
_____
_____
_____
_____
_____
_____
_____
_____
_____

Dr. Gritty

After reading Rodney's story, what did you take away and what can you implement into your life?

_____
_____
_____
_____
_____
_____
_____
_____
_____
_____
_____
_____
_____
_____
_____
_____
_____
_____
_____
_____
_____
_____

Chapter 2
S.W.A.G.

"Be yourself; everyone else is already taken."
-Oscar Wilde

Our young kids love October 31st. For us, it is just another day, but for them, the thrill of dressing up in costume and becoming someone else is exciting. They cannot wait to dress up as Doc McStuffins, Sophia The First, or a Teenage Mutant Ninja Turtle. You see, they love to pretend. What about you? Are you pretending? If so, then who are you pretending to be? Are you striving to be something you are not? For our children, acting like their favorite characters on television is adorable. However, when it's not Halloween, being something you are not is tragic.

Once the night has ended, together with our wives, we recap the night, eat some candy, have huggie time, a few kisses on the forehead, and then...night, night. That is Halloween for our kids and most kids across the country. The next day, it is business as normal. However, we have found that the concept of Halloween is more than a day for some.

Now, some of you never take off the costume. There are some students who spend so much time pretending to be the people they see on

TV, they have lost themselves. A few of you are trying so hard to fit in, you never stand out. Some of you are making decisions about your life, based on what you think someone else would say or think.

Like many students, we rocked Jordan's, two cubic zirconia earrings, and long chains with heavy medallions on the end. We could afford most of those items. Yet, when you put your swag in a car, you quickly find out your swag will not go very far. To sum this up, you can want as much as you want, but you cannot expect to have something you cannot pay for yourself, regardless of who has it.

Three-Point Star

While in our first year in community college, we had a friend whose parents were extremely successful. Our friend's dad was an accountant and his mother was a doctor. Needless to say, we lived totally different lives, and that was proven to us the first time he invited us to his house.

Rickey grew up in the suburbs of St. Louis. He lived in an all-white, two-story home that had four bedrooms which was located in the heart of a wealthy subdivision. His home was the type of home that two inner city St. Louis boys dreamed about living in as adults. It smelled new, looked new, and felt new. Rickey's home appeared to be 3,000 square feet, and it felt like the home had space for days. Do not get us wrong, Rickey's house was nice, but that was not what hooked our attention.

BOOM...BOOM...BOOM...BOOM...BOOM! That was the sound of the bass bouncing off the speakers to our ears in his Toyota 4Runner. It was all gray with black interior, a smooth ride. It was plain to see his parents had a little dough. Rickey's SUV had leather seats, a multi-disc CD changer, and two nice subwoofers in the back. What's more, it seemed that although Rickey did not have a job, he always had money to spend.

As the three of us would ride together to Taco Bell/Pizza Hut for lunch, he would play "Still Not A Player" by Big Pun, and the bass from his speakers would enter through our back and leave through our chest. Every day, for the first month of school, he drove his 4Runner. You could hear him at 9:50 a.m. on Monday, parking for his 10:00 a.m. class. That was about to change.

On this Monday, we saw a Mercedes Benz pulling into the parking lot. It was hard to see who the driver was because there was a slight tint on the windows. We stayed back as the car parked. When the car door opened, Rickey got out of the Benz and put his hands in the air and said, "What up, twins?" We could not believe it! It was one thing to drive a modest 4Runner, but a Mercedes?

For us, we just knew our friend was "rich." Rickey lived in a big house, parents had high paying jobs, he drove a nice SUV, always had money, and when he pleased, he drove a Mercedes Benz. We did not know any "rich" African-American kids our age. All in all, that made it more amazing!

Once our freshman year ended, to kill some time during the summer, we all applied and were hired at Sears department store. One Saturday night, we met Rickey over at his house and went to work together in his Benz. Once our shifts ended and we closed the store for the night, both of us asked Rickey if we could drive his car around the parking lot. He was fine with it.

We got the keys, one of us hopped in the driver's seat, the other in the passenger seat and we took his Mercedes for a test drive. From the moment we put the key in the ignition, we were going crazy! We were yelling and laughing as loud as we could. The both of us looked at each other and said, "We gotta get this!"

A few days later, with that twenty minute experience still on our minds, while driving home from work, we drove past a used car dealership in St. Louis city, and what was sitting on the lot? A 1991 gold Mercedes Benz 300 E, just like Rickey's. We turned around to see the car up close. It was gorgeous with all leather and the infamous Mercedes three point star logo embedded in the steering wheel. SOLD! We wanted it on the spot. How much was this beauty? A measly $8,000! What college kid does not have $8,000 lying around? "Yeah, we can afford that!"

After talking with the car dealer, we went home that night and numbered crunched for one minute. Then, for the rest of the night we talked about how dope it would be for our friend and us to go to the club in matching Benzes. We would be the hottest 20 year-olds at St. Louis Community College.

However, here is what we did not think about:

1. *How were we going to pay for it?*
2. *How many miles did the car have?*
3. *What was the car's history?*
4. *How would we pay the insurance?*

The fact was, we planned on quitting Sears before the summer ended and the only money we had during the school year was our $1,500 Pell Grant which came twice a year. Finally reality sat in. For real, $6,000 was not going to pay for this car when that money was supposed to help us stay out of mom and dad's check book, right? Well, who cared about that! One day, before we approached our mom about this idea of us entering complete ballin' status, we finally did crunch the numbers. After two minutes, there was no way we could pay for the car. So, we went to talk with our mom in the kitchen.

Rodney: "Hey mom!"
Mom: "Hey honey!"
Ron: "Mom, we want to buy a new car! It is a Benz, and it is really nice."
Mom: "How are you going to pay for it?"
Ron: "Well, we could use our pell grant!"
Mom, with the look of 'gimme a break' in her eyes: "What about your insurance?"
Rodney: "Can you pay for it?"
Mom: "You know your dad pays the insurance. And why would you want a new car when your dad just bought you a car before you started school?"
Ron: "Mom, this is a Benz not a Mazda 626!"
Mom: "Well, I am sorry baby, but you will have to talk to your dad about this!"

Dream shattered! Man, there was no more ballin'! Yep, back to being super lame and broke. There was no way our dad was going for this. It was not worth the time to ask him. Our Mazda was fine. We just wanted to stunt and make people believe we had more money than we had and we had none, with or without a Benz.

Our father purchased that Mazda 626 for one reason, to help us get our degree! It was certainly not to stunt, but to get something he and mom never received: a college education. Rickey's family was fortunate enough to buy that car. Good for him.

However, we were pretty blessed as well. Our father made sure our Mazda 626 was in great shape. Ok, it was not a Benz, but it got us from point A to point B. Hey, for what it was worth, we had a moon roof. At the end of the day, we worried about being something we were not. Cars, shoes, and smartphones do not make people any better or worse.

The both of us wanted to look good driving a luxury vehicle. We did not have a dollar to our name. If only we knew what we know now. The both of us did not understand what swag was as freshmen. We put our energy in the wrong place and it cost us time and money. We did not understand.

Understanding Swag

Before we explore the concept of swag, let's dig deeper with the definition. We heard swag was being confident, staying true to yourself, and creating your own style. In addition to creating your own style, swag has also been defined as the way one is presented to the world, to move with sophistication, and has an aura of comfort about oneself. All of those definitions regarding swag have to do with you taking ownership of you. Your presentation to the world illuminates your swag. When students do not recognize their personal swag, they forfeit their ownership to someone or something else.

Understand, your personal swag is to stand out, not fit in. There are roughly a billion people living on earth today, all with a different set of fingerprints. You are designed to be different. Some of our college students believe swag is being different from everyone else, but by pure nature, you are already different. Swag is being you, all day, every day. With true swag, you never and we mean never, compromise who you are by trying to be like others. Listen, this is not easy to do because we all want to fit in with our "friends." However, only when you are your real self does your grittiness kick in. Unfortunately, we did not possess this wisdom in our early years of college.

Time and time again, the two of us dressed like our favorite rappers with long chains, big medallions, and bandannas across our foreheads. We looked like cheap knock-offs! Our presentation to the world, at times, made us act and talk in ways, which took us from our true selves. Yet, we thought we had crazy swag! The focus should have been on our study habits and learning. But instead, we focused on having an 'image,' talking to girls, and hanging out with our friends.

By our third year in college, we dropped the "hip hop" look and wore what made us comfortable. In our hearts we were not street guys. We were just college athletes who enjoyed going to school and learning. It took us a few years to understand, but we got it. Later, as time would go on, we turned down the nightlife and started locking-in on our academic majors. Our grades changed for the better and so did our friends. We understood that our swag was already within us and we did not have to be anybody but ourselves.

Really, we cannot tell you how many students we have encountered over the years who have flunked out of college because they never understood the concept of swag. We have witnessed students simply settle for third or fourth best. You have to be willing to raise your standards to achieve your goals. That is swag! Remember, swag is ownership!

We are asking you to raise your standards, push yourself, and not settle for the easy road. We heard a smart man once say, "If you do the easy things in life, your life will be hard; but if you do the hard things, your life will be easy." If you can get an A or B in the class, why would you settle for a C or D? Better yet, if you could get an A, why settle for a B?

So why would a student settle? Settling does not take hard work. Settling does not require much effort and it is a cheap way out. We were mentoring a student who was on Honor Roll with a 3.2 as a freshman in high school. This high school freshman could have easily been a 4.0 student. But, this student settled for a 3.2 because it required no studying or preparation. We are not saying a 3.0 GPA is bad. That GPA is great if you can do no more.

For this particular student, a 3.0 was scraping the bottom of the barrel. Swag is being the very best YOU at all-times. Will the real you please stand up? We wished Katrina had stood up. She did not understand the importance of swag. If she did, it would have saved her time, money, and education.

Hurricane Katrina

Katrina was a student that Ron mentored while he worked for the Upward Bound college preparatory program. She was bright, intelligent, and ambitious. Once she graduated from high school, Katrina was accepted and received a tuition free scholarship into a local four-year university where she declared a major in business. With so much potential, her freshman year was a disaster. Katrina started the first semester by skipping classes regularly and focusing on her material possessions such as her clothes, shoes, and purse. Furthermore, some of her closest friends were not attending college, so she chose to hang out with them instead of locking-in on her studies.

After the first semester, her GPA was below a 1.49. Therefore, she qualified for academic probation. This type of probation meant she had the second semester to turn around her grades. If she did not make academic progress, she would be dismissed from the university.

Her second semester carried the same habits as the first. Not only was she skipping class from time to time, but now, she added a full-time job to her responsibilities. As a full-time student and full-time employee, something was going to suffer. Between her unproductive social relationships and a lack of prioritizing, by the end of the second semester, she was academically dismissed.

Katrina did not learn *The Rule of Transition* (See Chapter 5). The allure of her old friends, partying, "looking good," and working sabotaged her, academically. Like so many, she chose to simply fit into the crowd and be like her friends, instead of standing out. Katrina was under the impression that swag was restricted to fashion and the social scene. Katrina put on the "college costume." She had the books, pens, pencils, and class schedule.

However, she never fully committed to the process of being a student. A college student is not just about going to class, but it is learning and expanding your knowledge base outside the class as well. Real swagger is empowering and encouraging. Real swagger starts with S.W.A.G.

S.W.A.G.

New swag? What are we referring to? This has nothing to do with your physical appearance, but instead, it is the way you think in and outside of the classroom. This S.W.A.G. is truly taking academic and personal ownership. Unlike the swag on television, this S.W.A.G. will play an integral role in your academic growth. The swag in the media will have you looking nice, but this S.W.A.G. will help you achieve success in all facets of your life.

To use any swag, it takes 110%. But this S.W.A.G. needs you to rise and grind to reach your level of success. We call it your level of success because success, like beauty, is in the eye of the beholder. Listen, if you are willing to approach S.W.A.G. differently, there is nothing you cannot accomplish. With that said, let's get S.W.A.G.'ed out.

GRITTY.

Remember, most swag occurs when our students practice being something they are not. Now, we would like to offer you a different perspective. Look at it this way: S.W.A.G.=Students With Academic Growth. When we say growth, we are not talking about only classroom growth, but also outside of the classroom as well. Once you step foot on a college campus, the rest of your future life starts. Every decision you make will impact the rest of your life.

Remember this equation:
100 poor choices x 100 poor choices = a lifetime of misery and regrets.

It is not about making the "big, bad" decisions, but instead, it is the very small, "insignificant," "unimportant," "I can make it up next time" decision that causes so many students to fall short. For example, it is not the big Thanksgiving meal that causes unexpected weight gain. Instead, it is the daily dose of drinking a large soda, with weekly snacking on Snickers and chips, coupled with frequent fast food dinners. Those small choices, daily, and weekly will pay a huge price on the bodies of many people throughout this country.

This S.W.A.G. forces you to take your grades personal. You own them. It will be the sacrifices you make to learn as much as possible because with this S.W.A.G., your gritty thinking will help you to create successful habits which will last a lifetime. The small habits you learn will positively impact your grittiness. For example, looking at flash cards four to five times a day to study for a Biology test a week in advance; or the personal growth you accomplish when you spend time getting extra help because you are struggling with College Algebra; these examples can all positively impact your grittiness. The daily grinding and powering through will make you persistent, strong, and mature. At this level, you will tell yourself, "I will do whatever it takes to get the grades I deserve." Cheesy? Maybe. But this level of thinking takes grit.

Your high school swag was cool. It got you by. If you are a male, it probably earned you a few phone numbers from a few ladies. If you are a female, it most definitely forced guys to look at you twice. Your fashion sense was probably hot. We see you. Yet, your college S.W.A.G. must be about your performance in the classroom. Stay with us. If your hard work will get you an A, but you settle for a C, you have failed yourself. You… failed… yourself! We have mentioned settling once. It cannot be overstated.

GRITTY.

We took philosophy our junior year. In class, we learned about Socrates, Plato, and looked deeply in their ways of thinking. Snoozer! Time to count the sheep. We just coasted. There was little studying involved. We just went to class, tried to understand it, and when we did not, we went to the dorm and played NBA Live 2003. Not only did we play, we played the game all night. Playing the video game was fun and easy. We did that. Studying for philosophy was boring but necessary.

This S.W.A.G. was gone for this class. No motivation. We just settled for the C. However, deep down, the grade should have been an A. Take it from us, studying, at times, was extremely boring. Sitting in our dorm room or the library reading notes and/or memorizing flashcards made us want to fall asleep. Taking care of your grades and assignments are hard and necessary. Taking care of your business constantly will test your grit. If you are gritty enough, you will pass with flying colors.
Let's be truthful, we are not trying to hurt anyone's feelings here, but some students are simply copycats and frauds. For example, we see students all the time with the big Urkel glasses or dressing with the nerd look. Then he or she will claim, "I can wear this because I got swag."

That is the complete opposite of what we are saying today. Just because you dress like a "nerd," it does not mean you have swag. We are not knocking your fashion sense. We used to wear Timberland boots, a basketball jersey, and a matching bandanna (Yes, we dressed like that). Many have the "nerd" look going on. To each his own. But the grit shown studying, hustling, and grinding for every grade is your true swag.

Do you have true swag? Do you? When your friends ask you to hit up the club with them, do you tell them, "No thank you," so you can study for a test? If so, that is a **S**tudent **W**ith **A**cademic **G**rowth. Standing up and standing out, instead of simply sitting down and fitting in, is a **S**tudent **W**ith **A**cademic **G**rowth. There are many stars in the sky. But the biggest star, the sun, stands out the most! Be the flame in the classroom and set the world on fire!

When your swag transitions from fashion and friends to ownership, you have moved beyond what the average person is doing and you become amazing. This S.W.A.G. will have you writing a farewell letter to being average.

R.I.P. Average

Do you recall in Chapter 1 how we described our study habits for our political science test? We simply went to the guy that took the test during the class before us. We looked good in our jerseys and long chains, but our average way of thinking just wasted our time. We cannot successfully pass a class by studying the way we did during our freshman year. We were average students at best.

In biology, our study habits were worse than they were in political science. We did little to no studying in this course. We tried to charm the professor with our twin-thing, but she did not buy it. When push came to shove, our average study habits earned us a D.

If you desire this new S.W.A.G. you have to be willing to push past average. Why? No one likes anything average. Think about it, who wants an average job, with an average pay wage? Who hopes and wishes for an average car or house? Who wants to marry an average person? Today, people do not want an average cell phone. We would agree the average cell phone makes phone calls, sends text messages and has limited internet access, right? In reality, that is all people need a cell phone to do, but is it what most people want?

Today, we want a phone that can do more than the average capabilities of calling, texting, and web surfing. We want a phone that sends and receives emails, plays high-quality games, displays HD movies, responds to voice recognition, and video chats. The average cell phone on the market has no daylong press conference to announce its arrival to the average phone market. The average phone simply comes and goes.

Do you want to be that type of college student? A student who simply comes and goes? As we stated before, you do not have to settle. Honestly, you cannot afford to settle. Everything you are doing in school is preparing you for the future career you cannot see. If you have average habits now, you will have average habits later. Trust us, the competition in the job market today is tough and average will not cut the mustard. You have to be willing to do more in order to get more.

It would be safe to say some students' only study when a test is fast approaching. This method is an average way of thinking about college. No one should dictate your learning. Remember, a **S**tudent **W**ith **A**cademic **G**rowth is about taking ownership and growing into one's whole self. This does not just include the fashion aspect of life, it means education included.

A renowned educator stated once that living is learning and learning is living. The educator later explained that no student needs a professor or a teacher to tell them when to learn or study. You should be willing and ready to learn every day of your life. If Katrina had invested in her learning daily, she would have never been dismissed from school. With the tutoring and supplemental support colleges and universities offer, students should never fail. You do not have to be a genius to be successful in college, but you do have to commit to learning 365 days of the year. Trust us, there is nothing average about that commitment.

In our personal and professional years of assisting college students, we have found college is one of the only services young people would be willing to pay for in full, but only use half of the services. This has always been mind boggling to us. Would you ever consider buying a brand new car and only drive it half of the year? Would you pay your regular monthly cell phone bill, but only use half of the features or apps?

If you are paying for a product or service, you should use everything it has to offer. Like your cell phone or car, your college or university has different features to support you. Make it a point to use everything you possibly can on your campus. Paying for something and not using it to its full capacity is a waste of money and an average way of thinking. It is just getting by and you can't afford to just get by.

If you want more for yourself, give more to yourself. The both of us are fortunate because we were able to turn our college habits around. The partying, girl chasing, and hanging with the fellas changed into studying, preparing, and asking questions. Those qualities supported us once we started our core courses our junior year.

Master The Core

Arriving to Barry University for our junior year was something close to a dream. Living in St. Louis, Missouri since birth, we only saw Miami in movies and hip-hop videos. Once we arrived on campus, it felt like heaven. There were palm trees, students from all over the world, and beautiful facilities. We were lucky to say the least. The both of us declared as broadcast communication majors and were excited to get started.

However, something was different about attending Barry as opposed to attending community college. There was this intense focus to prepare broadcast majors for a job once we graduated in two years. Coming from a community college, we were not thinking about graduation, but exploring South Beach. We quickly learned going to Barry University was not about living it up on South Beach, but mastering the core courses to prepare us for life outside of graduation.

GRITTY.

The professors in the School of Communication expected excellence. All of them had worked in the field before teaching at Barry University. We remember our professor, Dr. Hoffman, saying to our classes, "First, if you ever get an A in my class, it is because you earned it! I will not give out grades. Most of you are juniors and seniors and many of you will graduate within two years. If you want a job in this profession, you better be top notch. I will help you get there, but you are doing the work." This was a new world for us. St. Louis Community College was rigorous, but nothing could have prepared us for the last two years of undergrad. To graduate with a high GPA, we had to buckle down, forfeit weekends and hanging out to produce the quality work the professors were expecting. We had to master the core.

If you really want to develop this new S.W.A.G., you have to put this concept in your spirit. Mastering the core is understanding your core courses which pertain to your major. For example, if you're a nursing major, you should be studying all of your classes, but especially in your nursing classes. Those classes will provide you with the essentials to be successful in your field once you graduate as a nurse. Understanding the core is the bread and butter to your major. Consider this, when you receive your college degree, underneath your name is a field of study. For example, (the

student) John Doe, (field of subject) Business
Administration.

By John having his degree in business
administration, this means he should have a
working knowledge of the business field. After
all, this is your livelihood on the line. Not to be
repetitive, but you are in college to learn new
skills and support people you have not met yet.
This understanding is the centerpiece to
everything you do.

No Pressure

"DRINK IT, DAVID! YEAHHHHHHHH,
BOOOOOOOOOY!" The boys cheered.
"Y'all crazy, dog!" said David with a half grin.
"That was nothing for me! Pass me two more
shots." We could look into David's eyes and
realize taking shots of hard liquor was not him.
He was not about that life. Dave was just trying
to fit in. This happens to too many young
college students all over the country. They are
showing their swag hoping to be accepted by
the cool group. You don't have to be something
you are not.

The key to college is not proving yourself to the
captain of the football team or the most popular
girl on the dance squad. The best part of
college is proving something to yourself. You
will start college as a young man or woman
and leave more mature and ready to take what

the world has to offer.

We earned Ph.D.'s in chasing pretty girls, we were masters at flashing our smile, and enjoyed the bachelor lifestyle. However, we were not into drinking and drugs. That has never been our thing. I know you have heard the drug talk since you were in elementary school. We will spare you. But in short, smoking weed and drinking until you pass out is not cool. Be bigger than the temptation around you. If you are hanging around drugs and excessive drinking, find a new place to chill, and different people to chill with!

Finally, attending college is not designed for you to make B.F.F.'s. If that happens, great! The purpose of college is to grow personally and to develop the skills to give back to the world. Truthfully, it does not matter what people think of you. However, it does matter what you think of you. Enjoy your time in college and the experience that comes along with it. Just don't lose "you" in the process.

White Music

When we think of someone who has real S.W.A.G., the first person we think of is Evan White. Evan took ownership of his education early. He never strayed away from who he was going to be. Evan graduated with his undergraduate degree in business administration. After graduation he discovered that although he liked business, he loved music engineering more. So to learn the game, he met with several individuals in the music industry. He picked up the phone and called music professionals located in different states. Evan had two part-time jobs and both were in the music industry.

These were not high paying jobs; these were entry-level positions which allowed him to get his foot in the door. With the money he made from his jobs, Evan purchased new music equipment for himself. He would stay up until 2:00 a.m. practicing music, go to sleep, and wake up at 7:00 a.m. to go to work. Evan's grind was like no other. To add to his musical repertoire, he paid for personal piano lessons. This young man was willing to invest in his own education outside the classroom.

After months of learning music engineering by himself, Evan decided he needed a more formal approach to his learning. He researched, contacted, and met with different music engineering schools. Finally, he decided to attend a school in Arizona. With his part-time jobs and financial assistance from scholarships, he managed to pay for a portion of the school in cash. Evan drove twenty-six hours to his new school and began classes in the spring of 2014.

GRITTY.

You see, Evan White did not stop learning
when he graduated, that is when his learning
began. We watched Evan get grittier after
graduation than during college. He kept looking
at the future and understood what it would take
to get there. You are no different than Evan.
This young man is the definition of S.W.A.G.
He did not fake himself as a business major.
He took continuous ownership in his learning
and development. Evan's ownership took him
from the Midwest to the South to study music.
That is S.W.A.G.!

Reflect

Who are you?

_____

_____

_____

_____

_____

_____

_____

_____

_____

_____

_____

Three-Point Star

Yes, we tried to stunt! Why do people spend their time "fake ballin'," instead of grinding out?

_____

_____

_____

_____

_____

_____

_____

_____

_____

_____

Understanding Swag

Explain three ways you can take ownership
in your life?

_____

_____

_____

_____

_____

_____

_____

_____

_____

_____

_____

Hurricane Katrina

Listen, we are leaders! If you met Katrina
today, what advice would you give her
about her future?

_____

_____

_____

_____

_____

_____

_____

_____

_____

_____

_____

_____

_____

_____

_____

S.W.A.G.

After reading S.W.A.G., you are starting to look at swag differently. What are the differences between swag and S.W.A.G.?

_____

_____

_____

_____

_____

_____

_____

_____

_____

_____

_____

_____

_____

_____

_____

_____

_____

_____

R.I.P. Average

Ok, you know exactly what it means to be average. List five ways you have been average so far. Then, list five ways you have been GRITTY.

Average Behavior:

_____

_____

_____

_____

_____

_____

_____

_____

_____

_____

_____

_____

_____

_____

Gritty Behavior:

_____

_____

_____

_____

_____

_____

GRITTY.

_____

_____

_____

_____

_____

_____

_____

_____

How do you stay gritty every day and move away from average?

_____

_____

_____

_____

_____

_____

_____

_____

_____

_____

_____

_____

_____

_____

_____

_____

_____

Master The Core

It is time to *Master The Core*. Develop a five-step plan which helps you prepare how you are going to master your core course work. Why is your plan important?

Developing your core:

_____

_____

_____

_____

_____

_____

_____

_____

_____

_____

_____

_____

_____

_____

_____

_____

_____

_____

_____

_____

_____

White Music

After reading Evan's story, what did you take away and how can you implement these lessons into your life?

_____

_____

_____

_____

_____

_____

_____

_____

_____

_____

_____

_____

_____

_____

_____

_____

_____

_____

_____

_____

_____

_____

_____

_____

Chapter 3
Know The Right Numbers
"When you know better, you do better."
-Maya Angelou

In May of 1999, the both of us presented our mom with a crazy idea. As a high school graduation gift, we asked our mom if she would buy us a cell phone. Having a cell phone was rare in '99. Most high schoolers had pagers at the time. So, having a phone put us ahead of the game. Today, things have changed quite a bit. As you know, smartphones allow us to surf the web, pay bills, play games, and tweet to the world. We are more connected than we have ever been.

Your access to information is at an all-time high. Here is the question though, what are you doing with this freedom? In a world of information, literally at our fingertips, we are using the power of the Internet for only social media. Let's be clear, we are not condemning social media. We are condemning social media if it comes before your education. Are you facebooking and tweeting throughout the day? During your spare time, are you sending picture after picture on Instagram? Have you memorized your followers on Facebook, Twitter, and Instagram?

GRITTY.

This is about the real numbers! Your Facebook friends and Twitter followers are numbers. The price of your LeBron's and getting your nails done are numbers. Do you know the right numbers? What are the right numbers? Good question! Knowing your Twitter and Instagram stats are not bad.

However, tell us this. How will knowing your social media numbers help you get an A in your hardest class? Will tweeting all-day help your GPA? When most of your attention is attached to your iPhone, iPad, or computer using social media, but you have no clue what your GPA is, how many credits you have until graduation, or what your grades are for the current semester, umm...Houston, we have a problem.

Last year, Ron was talking to a senior in high school. After talking with this young man for ten minutes, it was clear something was off. Just out of curiosity, he was asked what his GPA was; and he said the forbidden words, "I don't know." To push a little farther, he was asked, what his grades were in science, math, and language arts. He did not know.
Then, to be semi-sarcastic, he was asked how many friends he had on Facebook. Can you believe it? He finally knew something. It was a miracle! His face lit up, and he smiled and said, "500!" What about followers on Twitter? "A cool 300!"

The Numbers Don't Lie

Have you ever heard this quote? "Men lie, women lie, but the numbers don't." Wow, how true is that? Your GPA is typically a direct reflection of your effort in school. If a student had a 1.5 GPA, what would you assume about that student? Would you think that student studied often? Would you believe that student was passionate about his education? We would all agree that this particular student did not study very often, correct? This would be a safe assumption. On the other hand, what would you think about a student with a 3.8 GPA?

You see, you can fake your parents, you can fake your professors, but your GPA will not lie. Understand, your grades will not reflect your mastery of the class, but it does measure your effort. Allow your GPA to speak highly of you and your effort in the classroom. College is not designed for you to fail. If you need to raise your effort, get the help you need and understand the key numbers.

The Key Numbers

As you go through the college process, there are some numbers that are important to your college success. By knowing some key numbers, you can save time and money. We have witnessed many students fall prey because they did not have the right information. As we stated in Chapter 2, you have to take ownership in your education. Understanding the right numbers can assist with that ownership.

So often, students enter college and they are excited and geeked just to be there. Personally, we were not excited to be in college, we were more excited to graduate. Graduating with our bachelor's degree is one of our greatest accomplishments. We did not graduate college by accident. We were very deliberate with our studying, but more importantly, we knew the right numbers. Ok, what are some of these key numbers that should peak your awareness? First, know how many credits you need for your degree.

Don't simply attend class after class, without having an idea of how many credits you need to graduate. And don't just rely on your advisor to tell you how many classes you need to take each semester. Yes, your advisor is there to help and guide you, but not spoon-feed or hold your hand. You need to meet with your advisor telling him/her what you need to take in order to graduate.

As we speak with many college students, we listen to their stories. Nothing is more painful than a student being lost through the college system. What do we mean? We are talking about students taking classes, but did not have the proper information to make it to graduation. And worse, students get to the last semester of classes, but are unable to graduate because they are missing a required course.

Listen, your college or university is operated by human beings. This means mistakes can happen. Above all, your comprehension of your major is very critical. Don't leave your education in the hands of anyone but you. Your advisor, the dean, professor, and even the college president can help and support you. They can guide their students through the academic process, but they will not and cannot do it for you. Know exactly what you need, so you can get exactly what you want.

Next, understand the numbers behind the money. Like the classroom, the numbers that make up the money is your ownership. The financial aid office will help you get your money right. That is it. What you need to know is how much your education is per year. You should know how much because someone is paying for it. You would never buy a car and not be aware of the price.

The financial side and the academic side of your education are like a peanut butter and jelly sandwich. You can't have one without the other. Both the peanut butter and jelly need to work together for you to be successful in college. For example, you can't have all the money to pay for college, but don't have the credits to graduate. All the money in the world will not buy you a creditable degree if you can't meet the requirements. On the other hand, a 4.0 student that meets all of the requirements for graduation but fails to have the adequate funding to pay for school will not graduate either. Make sure you are constantly reviewing your financial aid to ensure you have the right numbers.

Lastly, know the numbers in the form of time. What are some of these numbers? Well, you should know when your school library opens and closes. You should definitely know these numbers during finals week. You should know the office hours for your professors and advisors. These individuals can help you to reach the next academic level. For real, you should keep their phone numbers on speed dial in your phone. These individuals are essential to your success. During our college days, our professors and advisors supported us with our credit report.

Credit Report

Everything that we are telling you has led to this right here: your credit report. As an adult, you will soon find out that your credit score is one of the most important numbers in your life. When your credit is high, banks are willing to loan you money for things like cars, phones, and homes. Conversely, when your credit score is low, banks look the other way. Your credit report is a summation of your financial habits. When we were in college, we did not have the concept of a credit report until we received a credit card for the first time.

During our freshman year, our dad decided it was time for his boys to take on some responsibility. So, he got us each credit cards in our name, but he co-signed. This meant if we could not pay the bill on the card, it would be Pops' problem.

Ahhhhh, our very own credit card. See, as 19 year-olds, a credit card meant everything was free! Here is how this worked. Once we got out of class, we would head over to Mickey D's, down a couple of double cheeseburgers, and we put it on the credit card. When we were dating the pretty girls and we had to pay for the movie, no problem, we put it on the credit card. When we headed to the mall and wanted a new video game, come on, we put it on the credit card. Ok, after two months of picking out free stuff from different stores, the bill came. Let's just say there were no bleeps in our house to censor our father's words. He told us:

"You don't have a job, BOY! I WILL HAVE TO PAY FOR THIS "BLEEP! "IF YOU KEEP ACTING DUMB WITH THESE CARDS, YOU

GRITTY.

ARE GOING TO RUIN YOUR CREDIT!"

We felt bad. Real bad! We did not realize that a few bad choices here and there could lead to a $400.00 bill between us. Our choices added up quickly. Those careless actions were not fair to our father's wallet.

Well what happens if you buy the wrong academic plan? What happens if you buy this plan consistently? You could ruin your academic credit report. What's that you asked? Your transcripts are your academic credit report. The grades on your transcripts are the result of the choices you made along the way. Here is the difference; your family cannot bail you out of D's and F's. Are you following us?

Every choice you make, in and out of the classroom, will have a direct impact on your grades. Regardless of your thoughts about your professor, your job is to learn. If you are not learning, you are wasting your time. If you do not learn, you will pay for it with bad grades. These numbers cannot be taken lightly.

Your teacher will still get his/her check deposited in the bank, and life will surely go on. You better own your grades. When your credit report comes out at the end of the semester, everything you see on it will be because of you.

Understanding The Script

There are areas on every transcript that you need to know. First, the name on the transcript. If your name is on it, then you own it! You have to be willing to take pride in your work.

Why should you take pride in your name? Because your name is a brand. Like Jordan, Apple, Sean John, or Nike, your name means something. For example, when you think of Jordan, what do you think about? You think of greatness, right? That is what makes the Jordan brand excellent. Now, what are the characteristics of your brand? What are people saying about you? What shadow do you leave when you are not in the room? Every time you sign your name on an assignment, it is like a professional athlete when her name is on the back of her jersey.

Professional athletes take ownership in their sport. If they do not work hard, they will not play, and remember no play...no pay! That applies to you as well. If you do not take pride in the name on your transcript, then your grades will never pay off for you.

But also, think about whose name is not on your transcript: your teacher! Every year the both of us hear the same speech from students, "The reason I got a bad grade in class is because the professor did not like me and she was too hard."

GRITTY.

We received poor grades in college because we were chillin' at the club the night before class. Poor grades were attached to our name because we were sleeping in class, recovering from the nightlife. That had nothing to do with the professor. We had to own our poor grades, no one else.

Trust us, blaming the professor when you are not studying is pointless. The professor is not at your school to like you, but there to teach you. The only way you will learn is when you take pride in your learning. The same way you own your smart phone or shoes, you have to own your learning. If you don't, you will most likely blame the teacher for your grades.

What classes are you taking? Do you know why you are taking those classes? While in our first two years of college, our academic advisor suggested the both of us enroll in easier courses. No, thank you! We knew how smart we were and wanted to push ourselves in the classroom. Remember, get informed about everything that applies to your degree. And if you do not know, it is up to you to find the information. That responsibility is not your professor's or family's. This is all you.

Finally, you are probably asking yourself, what does all this have to do with knowing the right numbers? The most important factors on your transcripts are your grades. Your grades are more than how you scored on a few tests and quizzes over the course of sixteen weeks. Think about it. Are your grades a true reflection of your effort? Sometimes the both of us earned C's in a course and it was the absolute best we could do. Other times, we received B's and slacked like crazy.

More importantly, your grades are the measurement of your progression and effort. Knowing your class grades and your overall GPA is critical to your success. You have to know what your GPA is every semester. Do you know your cell phone number, your address, or the year and model of your car? Yes? Then, without hesitation, you should know your grades! There is no excuse for students to attend class for four years and not constantly be aware of their GPA.

If you are already enrolled in college and you are reading this book, this is probably a refresher course for you. However, if after reading this and you have any questions about your own college status, we suggest you talk with your advisor. Remember, it is up to you to get the information and be aware that not knowing is not an excuse. Once you get your numbers in order, you need to prepare for the work that lies ahead.

The Rule of Preparation

So far in this book, we have been stressing the ownership of your education. This ownership will be the foundation for everything in your life. If you can learn to take ownership of your education, you will take pride in your job, relationships, family, and dreams. The both of us have encouraged you to seek the necessary help, stay true to yourself, and know the right numbers.

The rule of preparation states that everything you do now will impact the older you. For example, the 19 year-old you is preparing for the 30 year-old you. Understand? When we finally owned this philosophy, our outlook about college changed. You see, the 19 or 20 year-old you can't see the importance of the math or writing class. The problem is that the 30 year-old you will need that math and writing class to help you reach your goals. Realize the younger you does not realize the rule of preparation, so you decided to skip those classes. Therefore, the 30 year-old you does not have the necessary skills needed for the job market.

Believe it or not, you are preparing for something. The million-dollar question is, what are you preparing for? You are not going to class to just go. You are attending every class because you paid for it, but more importantly, you are giving yourself a better future. Again, what future? What type of future? Will it be a future filled with promise and optimism? Or will it be a future filled with pain and regrets?

Ok, when the younger version of you wants to skip class or not write the paper, just remember, you are setting up the 30 year-old you to fail. The 30 year-old you can only work with what your younger version has given you. If you don't give your older you an education, good work habits, and a positive mindset, the older version will be put in a difficult situation. Work hard now, so the older you can blaze a trail of success.

One Number Away

As you know, in his second semester in community college, Ron received a 1.7 GPA. There was nothing gritty about that. Little did he know, that 1.7 would make things harder for him in the future.

Late nights and missing classes will help anyone go from a 3.4 to a 1.7. Due to his poor decisions, Ron had to take summer school before his junior year. To make matters worse, he was offered a full athletic scholarship to play basketball at Barry University. Here was the problem, unless he successfully completed thirteen credits with a 3.0 or higher GPA, he could not accept his scholarship. To receive a 3.0 or higher, Ron had to take College Algebra. Math was not his strength. During his time at

GRITTY.

St. Louis Community College at Meramec, he took every remedial math course the school offered with barely passing grades. This is where knowing the right numbers are important. Ron accepted the challenge to achieve the required GPA to receive his scholarship. He knew the number of credit hours he needed to complete during summer school, and how long the math lab was open to students. All of the other courses were fine. Therefore, he focused on math. On the weekends, he would spend his time studying, locking-in, and completing extra math to increase his understanding. Ron had to make this work.

The young basketball player knew the numbers did not lie. If he did not pass his coursework with a 3.0 or higher, his scholarship would be thrown out of the window. For him, summer school was the fourth quarter with ten seconds left on the game clock. It was all or nothing. There were no additional scholarships on the table.

Therefore, if Ron had failed those courses, his college education would have been compromised. After all of the hard work, early mornings, missed parties, he did pass the class with a B+. Now, to simply get that B+, he sacrificed and put everything he had into that grade.

GRITTY.

In front of his face laid an opportunity of a lifetime. He could play college basketball and attend school at no cost in one of the most beautiful places in the world: Miami, Florida. His opportunity was almost taken away because of too much partying his freshman year. That 1.7 almost cost him everything. As stated earlier, the numbers didn't lie. Ron earned that low GPA by not going to class, sleeping while the professor was teaching, and having more late nights than early mornings. When things started to close in on him, Ron displayed a gritty mindset. Once summer school had ended, he met all of the requirements needed to attend Barry University for free.

The importance of knowing the right numbers can't be stated enough. If you are going to invest time and money to receive your credit hours, you better know what is required for success. Being gritty is being aware. You can't say, "No one ever told me that." If you are paying for it, the numbers are yours to keep. Those numbers could be credit hours, cost, and time. You own them all. When you own your numbers, you own your future.

You will learn quickly in college that you should be aware of your friends like you are aware of your numbers. Without being mindful of both, each can cost you your future.

Reflect

How many Twitter followers do you have?

_____

How many Instagram followers do you have?

_____

How many Facebook friends do you have?

_____

Now, the real questions:

How many credits will it take to graduate?

_____

How much will your education cost once you have graduated?

$_____

What is your GPA?

_____

The Key Numbers
Review your latest report card. What three messages does it say about you? Be honest!

Message #1

_____
_____
_____

Message #2

_____
_____
_____

Message #3

_____
_____
_____

Credit Report

As we told you, grades are a reflection of effort, not intelligence. If someone saw your credit report (transcript), what would they see and say?

_____
_____
_____
_____
_____
_____
_____
_____
_____
_____

Understanding The Script

In this section, we have informed you that you are a brand. Your brand is important like Jordan, Sean John, and Apple. In the business world, companies often do a S.W.O.T. *(Strengths, Weaknesses, Opportunities and Threats)* analysis for their organization.

Since you are a business (yes, you!), we want you to do a S.W.O.T. on your personal brand.

Answer each square honestly!

S. *(What are your **Strengths?**)*

W. *(What are your **Weaknesses?**)*

O. *(What are your opportunities for **Growth?**)*

T. *(What are your **Threats?**)*

S.W.O.T.

STRENGTHS	OPPORTUNITES
1.	1.
2.	2.
3.	3.
4.	4.
5.	5.
WEAKNESSES	THREATS
1.	1.
2.	2.
3.	3.
4.	4.
5.	5.
	6.

Notes:

_____
_____
_____
_____

The Rule of Preparation

What five habits do you have that will hurt your future?

1._____

2._____

3._____

4._____

5._____

Now, list five ways that you can correct these habits, so the "older you" can be successful?

1._____

2._____

3._____

4._____

5._____

One Number Away

After reading Ron's story, what did you take away and how can you implement these lessons into your life?

_____

_____

_____

_____

_____

_____

_____

_____

_____

_____

_____

_____

_____

_____

_____

_____

_____

_____

_____

_____

_____

_____

_____

_____

_____

Chapter 4
Play With Dogs, You Get Fleas
"False friends are worse than open enemies."
-Anonymous

If you have ever owned a dog or a cat, you know the real threat of fleas on your pet. As a pet owner, we will take several measures to ensure our pets are flea free. On the other hand, if our pets have fleas, we will do whatever it takes to remove them. When fleas are on pets, they cause the dog or cat to consistently scratch to deal with the irritation from itching. Sometimes, it takes several baths with special shampoo and medication to completely remove them. The irritation of fleas causes discomfort, which ultimately impedes their comfort level. Even though pets can't communicate verbally, we think they would thank us for removing the fleas from their lives.

Why are we discussing fleas in this chapter? Like our pets, as college students some of you have fleas in your life that will cause you to itch and scratch your way to success. Like animal fleas, your fleas are small and subtle and you don't know you have them until they bite.

So, what are your potential fleas? We define fleas as anything that will restrict, prevent, or handicap your success in life. With that said, you may have fleas as friends, family, surroundings, college freedom, or yourself. Yes, you may have fleas inside you. Do you have certain habits that are preventing or restricting you from achieving academic success? In this section we are going to focus on three fleas that affect college students more often than not: the Friend Flea, the Freedom Flea, and the Mental Flea.

The Friend Flea

Sometimes your best friend can really be your worst enemy. How? By hanging around unfocused people, it could make you follow her same path. You have to be careful how you are spending your time. The problem is that you don't know your friend is a bad influence until it is too late. Listen, we are not encouraging you to ditch your friends because you are attending college. We understand the importance of friendship.

Your inner circle is important to you. Got it! See, the friends that are focused and positive will support you through your educational journey. On the other hand, if your friends are hindering your growth, you should consider making a change fast! You are trying to make history in your life. Better yet, you are trying to make history in your children's and your grandchildren's life. You can't afford to let other people bring you down. The price is too great. Fleas are the people that are always around you, but their company brings more trouble than good. Like fleas on a dog, it is hard to get away from certain individuals. It does not matter how much you scratch; they are always there.

Here is a test we have used to determine if a relationship is worth our time. Ask this question, "Does this relationship add or subtract from me?" When someone is bringing you drama, day after day, that is draining and depressing. You don't need it nor should you accept it. How long do you want to itch? How long do you want to scratch? You have to get rid of the fleas in your life. The question is, how?

Have you heard this quote before, "It is a full-time job trying to take care of yourself."

What this is saying is that you have to focus on becoming a better you. To become a better you, commit your time and attention to your classes and your dreams. This is an old cliché, but friends will come and go. This is not being mean, but it is the truth. Will Smith stated, "If you show me your friends, I will show you your future." The people you are associating with are reflections of you.

GRITTY.

You need to befriend individuals who will understand and support your goals and dreams, not people that will negatively drive you down the wrong path. It is not fair to your future. Take a look at your five closest friends in your life, right now. What do they bring to your life? If you are willing to take a hard and honest look, you will be amazed at what you will find. Again, if your friends are ditching class, constantly in trouble with the law, and always having personal issues, the verdict is out. You need to change your friends!

To bring this point home, we would like to introduce you to Jason, a young man we have known since he was 13 years-old. Jason lived in an upper middle-class suburb and attended a highly regarded high school. He was good looking, tall, and one of the best players on his high school basketball team. When you say swag, Jason was the walking definition. His friends loved to be around him and the ladies loved him. As you can see, Jason had the world in his hands and had resources like his family, basketball coaches, and teachers. Unfortunately, Jason was infested with fleas!

One weekend night, Jason and a couple of his friends decided to rob an unknown residence in a very wealthy neighborhood. This was not like Jason.

Actually, he did not have to rob anybody. Jason's father owned a very successful business and his mother was in the financial industry. But sometimes when you are surrounded with fleas, you do as the fleas do. That night, Jason was the designated driver. Two days later, the police charged him with armed robbery. Luckily, he was a minor and was only placed on house arrest. He could only leave his home to attend school.

That is no way to live your life. Jason, like so many other good students, was saturated with fleas. As we have said time and time again, you can't stand out if you choose to fit in. Take a hard look at the people around you every day. Ultimately, you won't bring yourself down, but unknowingly, somebody else will.

Can't Change People...Change People

Once, we were working with a high school student who had all of the smarts and intelligence. She was tall, athletic, and highly capable. However, her biggest downfall was her clique.

Rebecca had swag; a ton of it. When she walked around school with her "friends," she would act tough with a bad mouth. On the flip side, when we spoke with her one-on-one, she was sweet and polite.

GRITTY.

In public, if her bad girl attitude was not enough, her grades were terrible. It seemed as if she was in trouble often for disrespecting her teachers. Daily, she was being something she was not. It was sad.

One day, Rodney had a conversation with Rebecca. It was clear she was struggling with her true self.

Rodney: "Why are you acting like this, Rebecca?"

Rebecca: "I don't know." She said with tears in her eyes.

Rodney: "Don't you realize how smart you are?"

Rebecca: "No."

Rodney: "Why are you hanging around your friends? Don't you realize that you are acting like them?"

Rebecca: "But Dr. Lewis, if I am not friends with them, they will talk about me. I don't want them talking about me!"

Rodney: "So...do you just act how they act so they like you?"

Rebecca: "Yes, it is much easier that way. Dr. Lewis, you don't understand. When they talk about you, it hurts."

A week later, two girls jumped Rebecca in the restroom. The following week, her parents withdrew her from the school. Rebecca, in front of her friends wanted to "keep it real." Yet in her heart, she knew she was not "keeping it right."

She knew those girls were bringing her down and helping her abandon her values. But, she settled to be on their good side rather than make the tough decision to separate herself from them. It is hard to make hard decisions! If you are going to be a college graduate and move on to bigger and better things, you have to make difficult choices about people. Sure, many graduates of college are dragging along unproductive friends.

We are not saying you cannot graduate. What we are saying is that this is a life skill and spans beyond college. Sometimes, the hardest choice of all is dropping friendships you once had. Can you still be true to your neighborhood, family, or friends? Of course you can! As the old saying goes, "If you can't change people, then…change people.

Remember, you have the opportunity of a lifetime in front of you. You know? You get to put yourself in a situation that will change your life. This is no time to blow it on toxic relationships. Once you establish your friends, next, manage your freedom.

Freedom Flea

Most high school students, when they are entering college, never consider the price of freedom. They get excited for this newfound freedom. In high school, teachers and parents strongly encouraged you to attend your classes. If you didn't attend class, your teachers and principal would contact your family. Your teachers and parents had a working relationship. This will change.

If you didn't know, this is the complete opposite of college. If you want to stay out all night, skip classes, and/or complete little to no assignments, that is wonderful; no one stops you. Yes, your family and advisors can share their concerns, but once you enter the big leagues, you have the freedom to choose where your time goes.

The reason we call freedom a flea is because freedom has prevented some students from being successful. We have witnessed honor roll high school students come to college and struggle academically. Their struggles were not due to the difficulty of the coursework. Rather, to the choices they made with their freedom.

Freedom is a gift and a curse. The gift is your independence. As a college student, you have the option to choose what you will do with your time. Once you enter a college campus, you are considered an adult. Mom and dad cannot call the university and check on your grades, unless you give them permission. You can add or drop any class you want. Ultimately, you have the power and the control over your education.

On the other hand, freedom comes with a curse. The curse is not being able to make the correct decisions with your freedom. We have seen more students waste their freedom instead of taking advantage of it. We would never tell you not to engage in social activities. There is a time and place to socialize and hang out with friends. The real problem occurs when you have no control or boundaries. Remember this quote, "If you abuse freedom, you will lose freedom." When criminals are placed in jail for committing crimes, they abused their freedom. Therefore, they lose what they once had. For college students, when you abuse your freedom, you will lose certain freedoms as college students.

For example, if you are on academic probation, you can't choose classes freely and may have to take certain classes to raise your grade point average. Don't let the gift of freedom become the curse of college.

If you want these fleas to stop biting you, then consider thinking about your priorities.

You didn't take out the student loan to simply waste it by receiving failing grades. Get your priorities in line with your goals. With your college education, you will have the opportunity to do more and give more than ever before. Don't waste your opportunity by having a "good" time. Trust us, when you graduate, you will have the opportunity to have a "great" time.

Common Thread

Every college student shares this one common thread. Despite your major, we all share the same thread. It does not matter if you have a 4.0 or a 2.0; we all have something in common. Regardless of your race, your parents' education level, or the country in which you were raised, we all share this. Every college student from St. Louis Community College to the University of Missouri has this in common. By now, you are probably wondering what the common thread is? What is it you ask? We all have twenty-four hours in a day.

In college, what you do with your time is so important. The question will always be: with whom are you spending your time? Are you chillin' with guys who brag about skipping class or girls who take pride in getting drunk? We are not judging. However, with your future on the line, you cannot spend your time with people or extra-curricular activities that will stop your success.

One night, during our sophomore year, we were playing NBA 2K. Minutes into the game, some friends called and asked if we wanted to go to a house party. Being the kings of the party that we were, we quickly got dressed and left for the night. Once we arrived, the music was blasting from the computer speakers and the girls were everywhere. This was our type of night!

As we went throughout the house checking the scene, something was strange. We could not find our two friends. The house was not very big and we wondered where they were.
As we walked toward the bedroom door, the smell of weed smoke rose. When we opened the door, there was smoke everywhere. The TV was on and our friends and his boys looked stoned times two.

Our friends were sitting on the bed, and once they saw us, one stood up and said, "Twins, what's good?"
Rodney: "What's up, man!?"
Friend: "Dog, for real, this party is crazy! Y'all want to hit that?"
Ron: "Nahhhhhh, dog we are good. You do your thing. We will holla later."
Friend: "Fasho! Y'all going to the club next week?"

GRITTY.

Ron: "We don't know yet."
Friend: "Aight! Twins, y'all stay up."

Our friend struggled in college. He never truly understood why he was attending school to begin with. There were times when he would show he was interested in college, but as time went on, his drinking and smoking consumed him. While we liked him, we made sure we did not follow in his footsteps and did our own thing.

And that is the key. You have to do your own thing. Do not feel pressured to do something you are uncomfortable with. We never drank in college, but time and time again, when we would go out to the club or a party, people would offer us alcohol.

We always turned it down. Neither of us are saints by no means. On the other hand, when you are in college, you have to draw your line in the sand somewhere. The both of us did not need to waste our time getting drunk. Understand that your time is your time. If you waste it constantly doing things that are unhealthy to your mind and body, in the long run, it will cost you. It may result in failing grades, tiredness, or disappointed loved ones.

Everything we do ends in a positive or negative consequence. Listen here, if you are using time for some fun, but mainly grinding for your grades, you are preparing for your future. Always remember, time builds habits. Make sure your time is used to build the habits that will help you graduate and start the life you want. Time is all you have and it is your most valuable resource. You cannot go back in time and re-do 11:00 p.m. in April once the time has passed. Follow your instincts about people and situations. If your friend is repeatedly saying hurtful things about other people, take your time somewhere else.

The common thread is the most important element of getting through college. In one year of college, you will have 8,760 hours to use. In four years, at the end of graduation, you will have used 35,040 hours. Every college student will get the same amount. So, the question is, what will you do with your time?

Mental Flea

More than the friend flea and the freedom flea, the mental flea is the most dangerous. Why? For some students it is too hard to change their own mindset, and they don't believe they belong in college. It is not about if you belong, instead it is about if you are willing to work hard enough. We have seen students fail their writing and math courses because they don't like to write or do math. It is not about whether or not you like to do math or write. It's really not!

More importantly, it is vital to your success that you realize you have to do the "hard and necessary" and not the "easy and convenient." If you can't write well that is fine, but don't complain and complain about it. Instead, take massive action and get the help that you need. If you have to meet your professor before and after class, then do it. If you have to visit the writing center five days a week, do it. You do whatever it takes without compromising your integrity to be successful.

The college process is like learning how to ride a bike. When you learned, maybe you had someone standing behind you as you were beginning the process. As you began to ride, your bike probably wobbled and you would occasionally fall down. Immediately, your guardian would pick you up, kiss you, and wipe the tears from your face. After a few minutes, your loved one would put you back on the bike and you would repeat the process. After repeating continuously, your guardian would move to the side. Before you knew it, you could ride a bike on your own.

Going through the college process is the exact same. You will fall over and over again. That is part of the process. We need you to get up, dust off your shoulders, and get on the bike. Your advisor, professor, and family members will hug you and help you get back on. So many students fall off the bike and never get back on to try once more. When you fall, you will do yourself an injustice if you just quit.

You are more than smart enough to excel in college. Truthfully, it takes time to learn the college process. It will be hard to learn the process if you don't hang in there and learn how to do it. We don't know any college students who have graduated without any challenges. You will have them, but you need to be strong mentally to handle your barriers and obstacles. There will be minor setbacks. Conversely, don't allow it to stop you from achieving success.

If you want to eliminate this flea, here is the cure: you have to be willing to change your mindset and believe. We have touched on this in the previous paragraph, but instead allow us to elaborate in greater detail. We are not psychologists, but from our observations of college students and our own college experiences, we know the power of a healthy and resilient mind. When our GPA's dropped as low as a 1.7, we could have thrown our hands up in the air and said, "We are just dumb basketball players; who were we trying to fool?"

"We are not smart enough to be in college." Yes, we could have quit going to class. Actually, we thought more like this: "This semester we screwed up, now it is time to get to work. We have no choice but to graduate; let's do the work." Listen, we are not saying we never had a down moment. The question is, how long are you going to stay down? For us, we could not afford to fail. We moved some friends aside and placed our priorities on our studies. Honestly, we just believed in each other and ourselves.

You have to believe in you. Again, you are going to fail a math test and/or do badly on a writing assignment, but you need to believe in you! Everything you do in college takes belief in your own abilities. When everything hits the fan and nothing is going right, we need you to believe that YOU will make it out of the storm. You will, but you need to believe you can before any action is taken. Your mind is like a muscle. As former college athletes, we know that if you don't build the muscles in your body, you will lose them.

On the other hand, if you lift weights consistently, there is no doubt you will get stronger. Listen, your mind is the same way. If you never exercise your mind with the weights of belief in yourself, then you will lose confidence in you. Like exercising, if you are willing to exercise your mind by believing in yourself consistently and often, your mind will get stronger. We would rather have a strong mind than a strong body any day of the week.

The importance in believing in yourself is crucial to your success. This may sound elementary, but the words are powerful, "If you don't believe, you can't achieve." Believe in yourself and you will build an extraordinary future.

Don't Keep It Real, Keep It Right

As we have worked with students from elementary school to college, we hear students say, "I keep it real!" We have found that this philosophy can be your own worst enemy. We don't want to beat a dead horse, but if you are going to college, you are probably doing something that no one in your family has done before. Someone, somewhere, is depending on your talent and expertise. Honestly, you do not have time to keep it real. On the other hand, you only have time to keep it right.

Ask yourself this question, "Why am I attending college?" Are you attending because it is the traditional path after high school? Are you attending college to make your parents proud? Whatever your reason, attending college is the right move to make. We have never heard anyone say, "I'm keeping it real, I'm taking four college classes." Have you?In some cases, this level of thinking is worse than having negative friends around you. You can get rid of people in your life. All things considered, that is easy. Yet, "keeping it real" is with you. And based on that thinking, you have the potential to make some rough mistakes.

It is not about keeping it real, but keeping it right. For example, if you write a paper and you put your heart and soul into the paper, submit it and receive a C-, you need to speak to the professor. During the conversation, your professor informs you that your writing is not college ready and the next paper will be graded harder.

Now, after leaving the conversation, you probably have real emotions toward your writing professor. You probably would like to drop the class or give the professor a piece of your mind. Those are all actions from real emotions and to be expected. The million-dollar question is: are you going to keep it real or keep it right? The right thing to do is immediately seek additional help. The right action to take is to go to your writing center on campus, allow them to read your paper, and provide you with feedback to improve your writing skills. Remember this quote, "Failure is simply feedback about your current skills." So if your paper was not high quality, then make your paper high quality.

College is not designed for you to fail. Remember the last chapter introduced a rule to you. If you don't complete the writing class, think about the older you. Don't say you can't do it until you have exhausted all options. This is the right thing to do.

By making the right decision, you are not only representing yourself, but you are also representing your closest friends and family members. You will learn in Chapter 5 that all of the hard work and effort you put toward your education is not for you anyway. Nevertheless, you have to be willing to do the right things at the right time. Your success will not be accidental. You will have to surround yourself with good people to help you reach your goals.

You Get What You Pay For

Remember the gold Mercedes Benz we wanted just to look big time? We thought we were going to pay for it by working at a department store. Yeah right! Once we realized that the car was never coming home, we enjoyed working that summer to earn a few extra bucks.

We worked together for the most part with Ron working in women's shoes and Rodney working in the children's department. Life was sweet. We had some pocket change to hit up the clubs and take our girls out. How could life get any better?

GRITTY.

The guys we worked with were cool as well. One was our Benz driving friend, and the other was Brian, who was a bigger club hopper than us. More often than not, when our shift ended on Saturday, we would clock-out and drive straight to the club with him.

One day, both of us noticed the guy who worked in the jewelry department about our age. He seemed pretty cool and would hang out with us sometimes. Brian told us about some things Chris was doing in the jewelry department. We were shocked! It was unbelievable. We thought, "How could the store let this go on?"

Chris was heavily discounting jewelry and cologne to his friends. When we say discounting, we mean discounting! For example, at the time, an average sized bottle of Curve cologne cost $40.00. After Chris would run it through his register, the bottle of Curve would cost $5.00. Yes, $5.00! There was a computer glitch on the cash register, which he figured out. Yet, Chris was very low key about his operation. He never bragged or gloated and was so smooth that we could not tell who was receiving the massive discounts.

Ding! "What if he could get us a few deals? Just a few! Maybe some gold and silver chains? Even better, maybe he can show us how to give discounts? Do you know how dope it would be to surprise our girls with new stuff?" The questions kept running through our heads. The idea of us learning this system became more intriguing everyday. For us, this meant we could get all of the hottest clothes, jewelry, and colognes for dirt cheap.

In late July, we were feeling like a million bucks! We had two big bags of clothes we purchased on our lunch breaks. We purchased $200.00 worth of clothes for a measly $20.00. As the weeks passed, we felt like ballers to the 4th power. We had sick clothes and eventually got the cologne and jewelry. The twins were set.

Although we knew it was wrong deep down to pay sixty-five cents for something that cost $79.00, the allure of having shiny watches and nice clothes was overwhelming. We were getting everything we wanted, and it was coming extremely easy. All good things come to an end, even this here. We learned quickly the truth in what our mother used to tell us. She would say, "Rodney and Ronald, there is always someone watching you." Her words could not have been truer. We were being watched!

On this particular day, Rodney was off and Ron worked. It was nearing the end of his shift and Ron went to get his check from his department supervisor. Once he saw her, Ron told her he was ready to pick up his check.

Ron: "Hey Cindy, I am here to get my check."
Supervisor: "Sure, Ron. But first, Bob wants to see you. Have a seat in my office."
Ron: "Cool."

Ron thought this was pretty routine. He did not think much of his supervisor's request to sit in the office. However, Bob was the store's manager. He looked at Ron and started asking him questions.

Bob: "Hey, Ron!"
Ron: "How is it going?"
Bob: "Fine, thank you. I want to ask you a few questions. How would you define stealing?"
Ron: "When someone takes something that does not belong to him."
Bob: "So, you think stealing is taking something that does not belong to you?"
Ron: "Yeah!"
Bob: "How would you feel if someone stole from you?"
Ron: "Mad."
Bob: "You would be mad if someone stole from you?"
Ron: "Yeah."
Bob: "Then, why are you stealing from us? Who else was doing this?"
Ron: "Just me."
Bob: "Come back here. I want to show you

something."

They got up and went to the video room. There, he showed Ron all of the footage of himself charging people discounted prices for hundreds of dollars' worth of merchandise.

Ron: "Hey, I will return the stuff. Can I just have my check and go?"
Bob: "No, the police have been called."
Ron: "WHAT?!"
Bob: "Ron, I will be honest with you. You are lucky you came to work today. If not, we were going to have the police pick you up from class."

Once the cops arrived, they handcuffed Ron and took him to jail. He was released on bond. Ron got a lawyer, and because his record was clean, the judge gave him two years probation. It could have all ended for us. While one of us got caught, we both could have been convicted felons. In hindsight, we should have never followed those guys in the store and recognized that fast money is not good money. But remember, when you play with dogs, you get fleas.

Please, do not follow our blueprint. The both of us thought we were invincible. Why on God's green earth would we think it would be okay for us to buy a $150.00 gold chain for $20.00? We were idiots. Nothing is free in this world and you work for everything you want. There are no shortcuts.

Know with whom you are friends. We knew Chris and Brian were good people, but the things they were doing on the job could have changed our lives forever. Also, those guys did not have basketball scholarships on the line like us. Compared to the life we live now, life as a felon would have been horrible!

Do not be afraid to say no when your instincts are telling you something is wrong. Listen to that little voice that guides you. And finally, do not worry about being called soft, weak, scared, or anything else. You are about to do something amazing; you are going to graduate college. And once you graduate, you will realize all of the hard work invested in your studies had nothing to do with you.

Reflect

This is important, what is a flea?

_____
_____
_____
_____
_____

The Friend Flea
Name seven friend fleas. Next to their name, why would you consider them a flea? (*For example: Allen-likes to get into fights*)

1._____

2._____

3._____

4._____

5._____

6._____

7._____

Can't Change People...Change People

Remember a time when you helped a friend do something wrong? What did you do?

_____
_____
_____
_____
_____
_____
_____
_____
_____
_____
_____
_____
_____
_____

Why did you help your friend?

_____
_____
_____
_____
_____
_____
_____
_____

_____
_____
_____
_____

What were the consequences of your actions?

_____
_____
_____
_____
_____
_____
_____
_____

Freedom Flea
Why is freedom a flea?

_____
_____
_____
_____
_____
_____
_____
_____
_____
_____
_____
_____

GRITTY.

How do you plan to use your freedom to help you succeed?

_____
_____
_____
_____
_____
_____
_____
_____
_____
_____
_____
_____
_____
_____
_____
_____
_____
_____
_____
_____
_____
_____
_____
_____
_____
_____
_____

Common Thread

How do you spend your money (time)? Review the table below. Pick a day and jot down where you spend your time. The next day, review it. What does it say about you? Be honest!

Where Is Your $ Going?	
Time	**What are you doing?**
5:00 a.m.	
7:00 a.m.	
9:00 a.m.	
11:00 a.m.	
1:00 p.m.	
3:00 p.m.	
5:00 p.m.	
7:00 p.m.	
9:00 p.m.	
11:00 p.m.	
1:00 a.m.	
3:00 a.m.	
5:00 a.m.	

What does your time say about you?

_____
_____
_____
_____
_____
_____
_____
_____
_____
_____

Mental Flea
What are your five mental fleas?

1._____

2._____

3._____

4._____

5._____

Why do you have these particular mental
fleas?

_____
_____
_____

_____
_____
_____
_____
_____
_____
_____
_____
_____
_____
_____
_____
_____

Don't Keep It Real, Keep It Right

Name three ways "keeping it real" worked against you?

1._____
_____
_____

2._____
_____
_____

3._____
_____
_____

GRITTY.

Name three ways "keeping it right" worked for you?

1._____

_____

_____

2._____

_____

_____

3._____

_____

_____

Chapter 5
This Is Not For You

*"The best way to find yourself is to lose
yourself in the service of others."*
-Mahatma Gandhi

We know what some of you are thinking.
"Going to college will make me a bunch of
money!" A lot of first generation college
students, like us, see college as a way of
earning more money. To be real with you,
attending college will make you more money, to
a certain degree. You are better off attending
college than not attending at all. That is for
sure.

Yet, going to college does not mean that you
will land a job that makes you $200,000 a year.
Trust us, this is not going to happen instantly.
This may sound lame, but honestly, college is
not about making money as much as it is about
you learning a skill to help others. If you can
provide a valuable service to others, you will
make money. That is how it works.

For example, many kids grow up saying they
want to be doctors and lawyers. They look at
those professions and feel doctors and lawyers
make a ton of money. They do! But think about
this. If you are extremely sick, whom will you
call? If you have to stand before a judge and
jury, whom will you call? What would you do if

these professions did not exist?
Doctors and lawyers are extremely valuable.
Medical doctors save lives. Lawyers help
people understand our country's complicated
legal system. They provide a service to people.
Do you get the message? It is not about you. It
is about the service you provide others.
Whether you are going to school to become a
teacher, accountant, or social worker, every
degree program is about providing a service for
people. Never forget your true purpose in
attending college. College is not about you as
much as it is about supporting others.

Each of us has heard students say they are
going to study high profile majors such as
medicine or law because of the money. Do not
be blinded by the potential dollar signs. On the
other hand, if you do not have any or have a
limited passion for medicine or law, do not
study those fields. Do something different.
When our daughters are sick, the last thing we
want is a doctor who cares very little about the
profession, but more about his wallet. That is
not right. The amount of student loans
accumulated from the time you start until
graduation will stack up some serious debt.

Paying off the student loans should not be a
problem if you have the grind and grit to work
and become an expert in your field. You cannot
do anything for the money alone. You have to
want it and want to be the best at it.

The Law of Transition

NEWS FLASH, this is not high school. You see, anytime you transition to a new level in life, you must adjust to the transition. The rule of transition states that you don't transfer your old habits when transitioning to a new level. Let us explain. When you graduate from a senior in high school to a freshman in college, this is referred as a transition. Every time you move up a grade level, you are entering a transition. Now, here is the problem for some students; they enter the new transition with the same habits from the previous level. We have witnessed students with 3.8 GPA's in high school that were on academic probation in college. Why?

Students tend to think college is a bigger high school. The coursework in college is far more demanding and rigorous than your average high school class. In high school, the ownership is minimum. If you skip class, the school will try to contact you at home or possibly contact your parents. College, on the other hand, rarely does anyone contact you when you are a no-show. Your parents typically can't contact the professor and inquire about your grades. This is a new ball game!

This law applies to all levels of college. Each grade is a different level for students. When you are on the freshman level of college, you can make "freshman mistakes." If you failed a class, maybe you can use the excuse, "I'm just a freshman." For some parents, making "freshman mistakes" are completely understandable. Those failures and successes are part of the growth of the college experience. Most of the freshman classes are 100 level or introductory courses while some freshmen are undecided in their major. On this level, people expect "freshman mistakes" to happen.

As you transition into your sophomore year, you must look at college differently. You are three years away from graduation; you can't afford to make "freshman mistakes." Your classes are 200 level courses that require more work per course. If you studied your freshman year, then you need to turn it up. If you are undecided, start considering a major. Get involved on campus or start to job shadow someone in your field of interest. Just going to class, somewhat studying, or chillin' will get you beat! We are not suggesting you don't engage in social activities.

There is a time and place for that. But now, you are a sophomore. Your mishaps as a freshman will not cut it anymore. Again, you are three years away from entering the "real world." Will you be ready? You need to start honing in on the future because next year is the money year.

GRITTY.

Your junior year is the beginning of the end. By now, you should have declared a major and taken your core coursework.

Remember *Mastering The Core* in Chapter 2? Now it is time to put that philosophy to good use. You should be studying hard to understand all the materials in your core. At this level, your freshman behavior is unacceptable. This level of preparation requires you to maximize your study habits. You are not studying for the class or the test, but for the expertise. Maybe, as a freshman or sophomore, you studied just for the test. As a junior, you are studying to own the knowledge you are paying for. This is the year to participate in internships and job shadowing. You should begin looking at the job market and deciding your future plans.

All of the hard work, pain, late nights, and studying has brought you to your senior year! Yes, you have partially arrived. We are saying partially because there's a lot of work that must take place between now and graduation. If this were a basketball game, this would be the fourth quarter. There is no crying or complaining, just simply doing the work that needs to be done. This year we are encouraging you to leave the parties alone. This year we are encouraging you to commit your being and energy to your major. Some seniors get lazy this year, which does not make sense. Think about this, why would you work hard for three years and slack off toward the end. It is go time! Your senior year is when you turn it up and get it done. This is not the year to waste.

If you have not been on an internship, this is the year to do it. Remember, someone is counting on you. Someone is depending on your hard work and effort. This is not the time to let them down. If you have been defeated prior to this year, it is the time to put the past behind you. You are a senior! What does this imply to the world? This implies that you are knowledgeable in your major and ready to enter the workforce. You are literally months from graduation. As a first generation college student, now it is time to take pride in this transition. Listen, there were numerous students who did not make it to this point, but you did. Be proud, but don't get satisfied.

This is the hardest transition to make because you have to remain motivated and hungry to reach the end. Also, you have to be prepared to transition to another level, earning a job. As you are seeking your first job, remember this law. Every time you transition to a new level, you have to throw away old habits and develop new ones. That is why this transition is important. Not only do you have to be concerned with graduation, but also immediately, you have to consider getting a job or attending graduate school. Whatever road you decide to travel, the law of transition will keep you sharp and aware of your surroundings. Look closely at your surroundings because once you graduate, you will start realizing that for someone, you will be a hero, which will make history.

Be Heroic

People have asked us why we do what we do. Yes, we do what we do for our family. We have to provide them everything that we envisioned for our lives. We want our children to have options in life and refuse to just live and accept what life has handed them.

One of our favorite heroes, our mother, told us, "No one will hand you anything in this life. If you want it, then you have to take it!" Therefore, we fight for each person in our household to make their life easier and will continue this until there is no breath left in our bodies. Yet, that is not the only reason we grind like we do.

Another reason is because we witnessed our parent's wake up in the wee hours of the morning. Our mom worked in a hot factory and our dad, in a kitchen. They worked five days a week with ten-hour work days. When we played high school and college basketball, both of them would be in attendance, screaming and yelling. They have done more for us than any other humans alive. We have to be successful and not only reach, but exceed our goals. They have sacrificed so much, that it would be a slap in the face if we had not pushed this college thing to achieve our goals! But that is not the only reason why we do what we do.

The major reason for doing what we do is because PEOPLE DIED FOR US so we can do it! People we will never meet, or never physically repay. These individuals gave their lives for us. They were willing to march, speak, and fight in the name of equality and justice.

They easily could have said, "This is not my fight. My family and I are living great and we are going to be fine." Nope. Instead, they said, "I may not be free, but someone in the future will be free." If slaves were willing to fight for their freedom, if Martin Luther King was willing to stand up to defeat racism, if Malcolm X was willing to instill self-worth and self-esteem into a group of people, if our mother and father were willing to pick cotton to support their families, the least we can do is get a degree.

This is light work. The least we can do is become the very best person we can be and take life as far as we can. These individuals throughout American history and our family history have left an impression on our minds, bodies, and spirits.

The both of us continually use their strength to help overcome setbacks and obstacles. Their sacrifice, their pain, their victory, and their success have been a major force in our lives. This is why you have to place going to college in the proper perspective. If you are like us, you watched someone in your life sacrifice everything for you. That person could have worked late hours and spent their last dollar on your clothes and shoes to make sure you were looking good.

The least you can do is attend college knowing the proper payback is your success through excellent grades and graduation. Compared to our parents' struggle and sacrifice, we had it easy.

Be Historic

An inspirational speaker once said, "You have greatness inside you!" We all have amazing gifts that only reside within us. Steve Jobs did not just leave this world an iPhone, iPad, and iPod. Instead, he left us his history, creativity, and vision. He left us his genius, which has changed the way most people use the Internet and make phone calls.

Martin Luther King left us a dream of equality and empowerment for all people. Dr. King left us his voice and his courage, which impacted millions upon millions of people around the world. This country is forever changed by King's intelligence.

What are you going to do to leave a mark on this world? What are you going to do to be historic? You do not have to make great speeches; you do not have to create anything new. Instead, give them the gift of you. Show the world your gift of speaking, writing, dancing, singing, rapping, video editing, drawing, painting, and the list goes on. Spiritual leader, Reverend Dr. Myles Munroe, believes you should live so phenomenal that when you die, you will have no need for a tombstone. That is a powerful mindset. He is suggesting you leave your imprint on the world so strong and powerful that people will always remember you. Come on, this way of thinking is on another level!

The homeless person, teacher, preacher, mother, father, everyone has the capability to lead their families, communities, and friends to a better place. All of us have the power and the ability to make history in our own way. Nevertheless, you can bless the world with your gifts and ultimately help someone else become successful. It is our humanly job to help and serve our fellow brothers and sisters. It is not just about you, it is about assisting others.

GRITTY.

Being historic is not about being rich and famous, but instead it is about recognizing that we have the ability and power to empower others. Thus, by empowering others, they will have the chance to empower others. Soon, it becomes a beautiful cycle of belief, faith, and fight. That is being historic.

Your gifts, skills, and talents are not for you to keep. The both of us are telling you someone is looking for you. Someone is screaming on the inside of their soul for you. Who is it? Who is watching you right now? Someone is watching every move you make and you are giving them the inspiration to keep going and never give up.

That is half the battle, leaving your mark on the world so someone else can benefit from it. This is what college is about. To help develop your knowledge, so you can leave that impression on the world. Simply, you should live full and die empty. What does this mean? Simply put, when we die, we should leave our knowledge and gifts with the world.

What is the richest place on the earth? It is not the gold mines, it is not the diamond mines in Africa, nor is it Oprah's house. It has been stated that the richest place in the world is the cemetery. Now wait, you may be thinking, the cemetery!? Yes, the place your body goes when your time is up.

You see, in the cemetery lies books unwritten, songs that cannot be released to the world, inventions that were never found to cure diseases. If we do not leave our gifts with the world, all of us miss the opportunity to impact someone else's life. Whatever gift you have, it is meant to be released back to the people. If you have a beautiful voice, then let the world hear you sing!

Sing so loud and proud that the world can benefit. Who knows, it might be the way you sing a song that might get a person through a rough time. As we have stated over and over, this has nothing to do with you in the grand scheme of life. You are supposed to have the talent because that is how it was written. Listen closely, you are so important, that talent was given to you to impact the world. So, get straight A's, help a struggling classmate, and/or study extra hard. Just understand, the more knowledge and talent you have, the more you can give away. And that makes history!

Walk A Mile In Her Shoes

One inspirational person the both us look up to is our younger sister, Angela Lewis. Angela understands the concept of this chapter very well. She is a walking illustration and an example of the power of giving. Everything she has accomplished thus far, she knows it will better humanity. She studied communication at St. Louis University. With her education, she has authored a book and has developed herself as an influential author and speaker, nationally. Her book, *The Game Changing Assist*, is about helping others, and when she speaks to college athletes or young women, her goal is to use her gifts to support others. She is one of the most genuine people we know.

One of her biggest accomplishments is organizing a shoe drive for the citizens in Kenya, Africa. Since 2011, Angela has been organizing this shoe drive. Through generosity from friends and colleagues, she was able to provide three shipments of shoes and clothes to families in Kenya. In 2013, she doubled her initial shipment. Her goal is to visit Kenya, Africa in the near future to find additional ways to assist and support their community.

This story was not told to you to brag or boast about our sister. On the other hand, you are hearing this because she is a great example of why your education is not for you. Angela did not have to start a shoe drive for families in Kenya. Honestly, she has plenty of things she could do with her time. Throughout this chapter, you have been reminded that your education is for someone else. Your degree will allow you to serve others, using your time, abilities, and your expertise. Angela used her communication degree for writing and speaking to support the hopes and dreams of other people. She uses her communication skills to deliver a powerful message to her friends and colleagues of the shortage of shoes in that country. Angela lives in Missouri, but she is speaking on behalf of Kenyan residents. That is amazing!

When you feel like giving up, hold on just a little longer. Listen, somebody needs you to complete your college education. We need you to be willing to stand up and use your knowledge and expertise to fight for them. The more you know, the more you can give. You have to be willing to learn more and more, so you can make someone else's life better. You never know when you will be called to share your knowledge. If Angela had not mastered the core, she never would have been able to convey a powerful message on behalf of the citizens in Africa. She will forever be heroic and historic because she dedicated her time, energy, and education to make the world a better place. Your education is not for you!

Reflect

What is your number one reason for pursuing your dreams?

_____
_____
_____
_____
_____

The Law of Transition
What five habits do you have, right now, that will hurt you in the future?

1._____

2._____

3._____

4._____

5._____

Be Heroic
Name three heroes in your life?

1._____

2._____

3._____

How have these heroes been instrumental
in your life?

_____
_____
_____
_____
_____
_____
_____
_____
_____
_____
_____
_____
_____
_____
_____
_____
_____
_____
_____
_____
_____
_____
_____
_____

GRITTY.

What three qualities do your heroes share
in common? Why are they heroic to you?

1._____

_____

2._____

_____

3._____

_____

_____

_____

_____

_____

_____

_____

_____

_____

_____

_____

_____

_____

_____

_____

_____

_____

_____

Be Historic

How will you leave your mark on the world?

_____

_____

_____

_____

_____

_____

_____

_____

_____

_____

_____

_____

How will your mark impact the world?

_____

_____

_____

_____

_____

_____

_____

_____

_____

_____

_____

_____

_____
_____
_____
_____
_____
_____
_____
_____

Why is leaving your mark important to the world?

_____
_____
_____
_____
_____
_____
_____
_____
_____
_____
_____
_____
_____
_____
_____
_____
_____
_____
_____

Walk A Mile In Her Shoes

After reading Angela's story, what did you take away and how can you implement these lessons into your life?

_____

_____

_____

_____

_____

_____

_____

_____

_____

_____

_____

_____

_____

_____

_____

_____

_____

_____

_____

_____

_____

_____

_____

Chapter 6
Make It Count

"Nobody can give you wiser advice than yourself."
-Marcus Tullius Cicero

Your cap... thrown, gown... worn, and graduation... commenced, now what? Yes, you excelled in your courses and earned a high GPA. What's next? The job market should offer you opportunities left and right, correct? If you want a job once you graduate, then turn on your grit, roll up your sleeves, and get ready to work. It will not be easy. And many times the pain and rejection will cause a tear. But with every, "Hello, we are moving forward with another candidate" speech, your grittiness, or your resilience to overcome, will force you to dust yourself off and try again. In order to land that job, it will be determined by your belief, ability to connect, and fight you have to overcome the rocky road to employment. Only you can make this happen.

Believing

If you do not believe in your skills, talents, and abilities, then forget about the job. You will not have a chance. Think about it, the marketplace is saturated with competition. Why would an organization have confidence in you, if you do not have confidence in yourself? Come on, if a

Take advantage of your professors' knowledge. It will not be there forever. Take advantage of the relationships you gained with friends. They will not be there forever. Take advantage of your experiences such as the classes you take and new places you are exposed to. They will not last forever.

College is not about attending school and earning 4.0's. Attending college is about the preparation of life. You can only stay in this preparation for so long; it has to end. For us, ten years ago, we rarely thought about life in these terms. Maybe if we had, some of our poor choices would have been different. However, we are glad we experienced those difficulties and defeats because now we have an opportunity to prepare you for the road ahead. Live with purpose, passion, and presence. You should! Why? Because...you will not be here forever.

We Are Just Like You

Finally, if you have ever felt pain and rejection, we are just like you. Those 14's we earned on our ACT made us feel like idiots. We had to grind through our thoughts of stupidity to excel in community college. We got gritty! If you come from a community of violence, drugs, and gangs, we are just like you. If you ever thought you were not as smart as your classmates, we are just like you.

GRITTY.

Despite it all, we made it through bad grades. The both of us are earning doctorates and writing a book. If we can go from 14's on the ACT and get doctorates, you can do anything. If we can go from 1.7's and 2.3's to 4.0's, you can accomplish whatever your heart desires. Yes, you can make your dreams come true. Do not let grades, GPA's, and high stakes tests define you. You are bigger and more powerful than the numbers attached to your name.

We have come a long way from two chubby little twins from St. Louis, Missouri. Sometimes, it is hard to believe we are writing a book. The twins are writing a book! The twins, who hated to read and could not write a lick. If we can write a book, you can overcome your pain and graduate from college. You can be everything you ever wanted because if we can do it, you most certainly can do it.

Without a doubt, that is what it means to be Gritty!

Reflect

Ok, you are graduating from the big leagues, what's next? Keep your number one goal in mind. What is that goal?

_____

Believing
What are the top three skills or abilities you have to offer an employer?

1._____
_____

2._____
_____

3._____
_____

How many people in your field are aware about these skills you embody?

_____
_____
_____
_____
_____
_____
_____
_____

Connecting

Name five professionals you know in your field?

1._____

2._____

3._____

4._____

5._____

Do the contacts above "know you?" Please circle: YES or NO

If you circled NO, why not?

_____
_____
_____
_____
_____
_____
_____
_____
_____
_____
_____
_____

If you circled YES, how can you strengthen the relationship?

_____
_____
_____
_____
_____
_____
_____
_____
_____

Fighting
List the top five companies that you want to work for in the future?

1._____

2._____

3._____

4._____

5._____

_____
_____
_____
_____

Now, write down five people, companies, phone numbers, and email addresses of individuals in your industry.

Get Connected!

Contact Person	Company	Phone # and Email

Lastly, regardless if you know the contacts or not, when are you going to call them and schedule a time to meet?

Due Date:_____

We Are Just Like You
What are three major failures in your life?
Why are they failures?

1._____
_____
_____
_____
_____
_____
_____
_____

2._____
_____
_____
_____
_____
_____
_____
_____

3._____
_____
_____
_____
_____

_____
_____
_____

What are five reasons, without a doubt, you will overcome the odds stacked against you?

1._____

2._____

3._____

4._____

5._____

Success sucks! If you really want to tackle success, you must plan for it!

Write down your top short term, mid-term, and long term goals. Start planning and think big!

Short Term Goals (1-6 months):

1._____

2._____

3._____

How are you going to achieve them?

_____
_____
_____
_____
_____
_____
_____
_____
_____
_____
_____
_____
_____
_____
_____
_____
_____
_____
_____
_____
_____

GRITTY.

Mid-term Goals (1-4 years):

1._____

2._____

3._____

How are you going to achieve them?

GRITTY.

Long Term (5-20 years):

1._____

2._____

3._____

How are you going to achieve them?

_____
_____
_____
_____
_____
_____
_____
_____
_____
_____
_____
_____
_____
_____
_____
_____
_____
_____
_____

My Hustle
By: The Lewis Influence

This is it, I won't quit, it is my time.... hustle
I am in a valley, I am about to climb.... hustle

I have come too far, not to shine.... hustle
Trust us, no days off, grind.... hustle

I am living with my eyes closed, blind.... hustle
This is rooted in pain, where you find.... hustle

I am never giving up, I have strong.... hustle
In it until I win it, baby, long.... hustle

This is study hustle, learning.... hustle
This is bloody hustle, this is burning.... hustle

Mom and dad, I want to make you proud....
hustle
Voice my dreams to the world, loud.... hustle

Stand toe to toe with fear, no fear.... hustle
The haters say we can't, we can't hear.... hustle

When the failure approaches us, no tear....
hustle
This is real, nothing fake, sincere.... hustle

Look at my child, this is not for me.... hustle
Going harder, my vision I can see.... hustle
We can't be normal, average is dead.... hustle

GRITTY.

You value your gift, heard what I said.... hustle

Victory is near, baby I am focus.... hustle
No smile on face, not joking hustle.... hustle
Keep running until you make it to the top....
hustle

Volunteer people and keep giving.... hustle
Make your mind up, show time decision....
hustle

Waking up at 3, never get tired.... hustle
I will sleep when I am dead, that is retired....
hustle

I am doing it now, I am done with try.... hustle
This is Lewis Influence, and.... my hustle

Acknowledgements

Every morning, mom and dad would wake up early and head off to work. Mom had two jobs. By day, she worked in a hot and uncomfortable factory. By night, she was taking care of three attention-seeking kids who loved to jump, run, and play. Mom prepared the meals, washed the dishes, ironed the clothes, and cleaned the house. She did everything. Mom never complained. As we got older, we realized our amazing mother did all of that, every day, for us. This woman only had an elementary education, and is one of the smartest women we know. This book is for her! She is gritty, and our hero helped us form a "never quit" attitude.

Mom, your boys love you! Thank you for supporting us for thirty three years. This book is for you.

The other half of that equation is "big poppa" as we call him from time to time. Dad is a "man's man." He taught us to "handle our business first, and always play second." Like mom, he had two jobs as well. However, most of his days were spent at the bakery. This high school dropout started out mopping floors and worked his way up to lead chef. Literally, our dad taught himself everything there is about being a chef. That is grit in its truest form. His self-discipline and integrity is second to none, and he instilled those values into his twin boys with big dreams.

Dad, your boys love you! Thank you for teaching us to be a "man!" This book is for you!

You cannot think about Rodney and Ron without Angie! Our sister is the epitome of class. As the author of *The Game Changing Assist,* she has changed the lives of girls and student-athletes all over the country. Angie is amazing at bringing people together and making them feel worthy. Everyone does not have that quality. Single handedly, she is the reason why the birth of this book has taken place. When we held her first book in our hands, she made the thought of becoming an author, real.

Angie, you are simply amazing! Thank you for being you! This book is for you!

We love each of you so much!
-Rodney and Ron

Acknowledgements from Rodney:

Crystal, thank you for your unconditional love and support. Without a doubt, I know you were made for me. Sophia, can you believe it baby? Uncle Ron and daddy are authors! I love you so much princess. I will buy you something from the Slushie Store (Target)!

To all my friends and colleagues, I personally thank you for the unwavering encouragement and support.

Acknowledgements from Ron:

Elisa, thank you so much for pushing and encouraging me to live my dreams. With your support, I was able to write this book from my heart. I know I have sacrificed time with our family, but I will be forever indebted to your love and support.

Issac, Damon, Tyson, Sebastian, and Emerson, you guys are simply brilliant! Words can't describe the feeling I receive when I see your faces. I want to give you the best and brightest future I possibly can. Thank you for loving me for me. Daddy loves you!

To all my friends and colleagues, I personally thank each of you for the unwavering encouragement and support.

About The Authors

Dr. Rodney and Ron Lewis are the founders of The Lewis Influence, an organization designed to give first generation college students the tools they need to be successful before, during, and after college.

The mission of The Lewis Influence is to provide guidance and inspiration to first gen students throughout the world.

Rodney and Ron, both first generation college students, received full basketball scholarships to play for St. Louis Community College at Meramec and Barry University.

GRITTY.

They both would graduate with their bachelor's degree in broadcast communication.
Later, both would receive their master's degree. Rodney earned two masters degrees, one in Teaching and the other in educational administration. Ron, received his master's degree in sports management from Barry University.

In 2010, Rodney graduated from Maryville University with his doctorate in educational leadership. Ron is currently pursuing his Ph.D. in global leadership from Indiana Tech University.

Currently, Rodney is the principal of an elementary school in the Rockwood School District in St. Louis, Missouri. Ron is the Director for the TRiO Student Support Services program at the University of St. Francis in Fort Wayne, IN.

This dynamic duo is passionate about the achievements and success of all first generation college students across the world.

GRITTY.

How to sign up for Dr. Influence's My
First Class messages:

To receive messages via text, text
@drinf to (224) 231-5038. You can
opt-out of messages at anytime by
replying, 'unsubscribe @drinf'.

*Standard text message rates apply

Or to receive messages via email, send
an email to drinf@mail.remind101.com.

First gen students, do you want
the Lew Flu weekly? You got it!
Now, you can receive weekly
text messages by taking 5
seconds to sign up.

We do not collect personal
information, we just give
inspiration.

Sign up today!

Connect

Website
www.lewflu.com

Twitter
@firstgentwins

Facebook
www.Facebook/lewisinfluence

Instagram
@lewflu

Email
lewisinfluence@gmail.com

GRITTY.

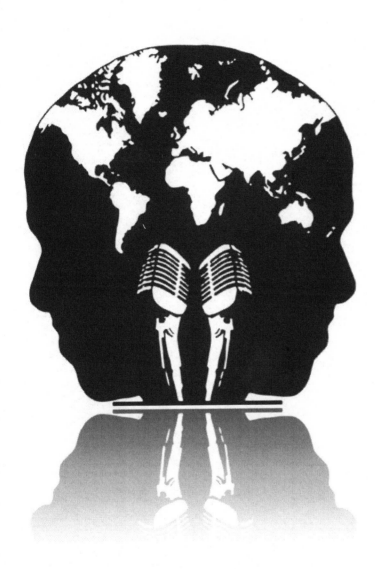

GRITTY.